Turn page →

Passion on Purpose

FOCUS ON THE FAMILY®

Turn the page →

Passion on Purpose

Discovering and Pursuing a Life that Matters

Dr. Deborah Newman

TYNDALE

Tyndale House Publishers, Wheaton, Illinois

Passion on Purpose
Copyright © 2003 by Deborah Newman
All rights reserved. International copyright secured.

ISBN: 1-58997-126-4

A Focus on the Family Book published by
Tyndale House Publishers, Wheaton, Illinois 60189
Renewing the Heart® is a registered trademark of Focus on the Family.

All Scripture quotations, unless otherwise indicated, are taken from the *Holy Bible, New International Version*®. NIV®. Copyright © 1973, 1978, 1984 by International Bible Society. Used by permission of Zondervan Publishing House. All rights reserved.

The case examples presented in this book are fictional composites based on the author's clinical experience with hundreds of clients through the years. Any resemblance between these fictional characters and actual persons is coincidental.

Focus on the Family books are available at special quantity discounts when purchased in bulk by corporations, organizations, churches, or groups. Special imprints, messages, and excerpts can be produced to meet your needs. For more information, contact: Resource Sales Group, Focus on the Family, 8605 Explorer Drive, Colorado Springs, CO 80920; or phone (800) 932-9123.

Editors: Kathy Davis and Liz Duckworth
Cover Design: Amy Kiechlin

Library of Congress Cataloging-in-Publication Data
Newman, Deborah.
    Passion on purpose : discovering and pursuing a life that matters / Deborah Newman.
       p. cm.
Includes bibliographical references.
    ISBN 1-58997-126-4
    1. Christian women—Religious life. I. Title.
    BV4527 .N465 2003
    248.8'43—dc21

                                                                2003001350

Printed in the United States of America
1 2 3 4 5 6 7 8 9 / 09 08 07 06 05 04 03

whose enthu

Contents

�֎

Acknowledgments

✿

Thank you to Focus on the Family Product Development for believing in this message and giving me a venue for sharing it. Mark Maddox, Kathy Davis, Liz Duckworth, Stacey Herebic: You do your part faithfully. I'm blessed to be associated with Tyndale House Publishers and appreciate their diligence in marketing and publishing.

I want to recognize the "Tea Time for Your Soul" readers who encouraged me to write a book from the series of articles I did several years earlier. A very special thank you goes to Brenda Mammel for letting me share her personal letter to me in this book.

Although all the stories in this book are based on fictional people and events, I want to thank all the people who have sat in my counseling office and opened their lives to me. I've learned so much from each of you and acknowledge how you have helped me better communicate the points I'm trying to make.

Brian, you are the wind beneath my wings. Rachel and Ben, you help me be accountable in how I live my life. The three of you bring so much meaning to my life.

Finally, I thank God for giving me such abundant opportunities to share what He's shown me about pursuing a life full of meaning and purpose. It is a privilege to belong to Him.

Introduction

❦

What do you have to say about your life?

I long for the day when a friend asks me how I'm doing and I can reply, "I'm doing all the things that God wants me to be doing." Instead, my usual answer is, "I am busy." I respond that way because to honestly share about what I am really doing would take half an hour, and I know that's not what my friend wants to hear.

I used to be proud to say, "I am busy," as if being busy meant I was living well—that I was important and valuable because I had a lot to do. I don't think that way anymore. I realize that I can be the busiest person at my church or office yet still not be doing what is most important in my life.

My prayer for this book is that it will be a guide to help women examine the busyness of their lives. I hope it will reveal how to find a fulfilling life, a life full of meaning and purpose. Ideally, I'd love to encourage women to read this book in a small group or in a one-on-one discipleship relationship. Most of us need to take a good long look at our lives and discover what is really important. To do this most effectively we often need a friend to walk with, one who will point out strengths we didn't notice or weaknesses we would rather not face. The appendix provides guidelines and suggestions for using this book in a small-group Bible study or for a one-on-one discipleship relationship.

Journal Exercises

At the end of each chapter you will find journal exercises. Please don't skip over the exercises. They provide essential steps to discovering and pursuing a life that matters. After reading the chapter, give yourself time to think through the questions in each journal exercise.

1

Goal for the Week

The goals for the week are easy, practical challenges to keep your mind centered on what you've read. They act as daily reminders about the changes you are making.

You will get the greatest benefit from this book if you make some preparations. If it is your desire to definitely pursue a life full of meaning and purpose, you can't just read these words; you need to follow up on the instructions given in each chapter. Here are some guidelines to follow in addition to reading:

First, find a journal in which to compose your personal thoughts. You can use your journal to complete the journal exercises at the end of each chapter. Also use your journal to record your thoughts to God about how you are living your life. Reflecting on your life is important if you are going to make meaningful changes, and this book will give you opportunities to think about your life, your feelings, and your relationships. Keep a record of your progress, and try to reread your journal at least monthly. Sometimes you might miss what God is saying to you, but reviewing your journal will help you catch what you missed the first time.

Second, find a friend to share this journey. Women grow, heal, and change through relationships, and relationships are central to who we are and how God made us. (For more on this read *A Woman's Search for Worth*.[1]) You will receive the most benefit from this study if you have someone with whom to share your hopes, fears, and dreams. (Though its primary focus is women, this book is also useful for married couples seeking to grow in their lives together.)

Third, set aside a specific time on your calendar to read each chapter. I hope you won't just read this book and then put it on the shelf; I'm praying that it will become a tool to help you hear what God has to say about your life. I recommend you read only one chapter a week, taking time to thoroughly think through the issues addressed. Make appointments with your study group or partner to review what you have learned on a weekly basis. Make appointments with yourself to have time for reflection and reading. Believe me, your busy life will take over, and you will never find the time to make meaningful changes unless you decide it is important and follow through by making it a priority on your calendar.

Fourth, keep your commitments to change. Changing your life doesn't happen overnight. It happens in the small decisions you make. You will not reach your dream life by the end of the book, but you will be much closer to it than to your old life if you will do the "small stuff." Take it one step at a time. Don't be a perfectionist, saying, "If I can't be a super saint in two years, why try?" If you commit to making small changes, the fruits will be well worth the effort.

Fifth, celebrate the changes. You need someone who can be happy for you when you make a simple decision that was difficult for you. You need someone to make a big deal out of it. This is why it is so helpful to have a partner on your journey. You also need to make a big deal of it yourself. As you will learn, we have a God who rewards us. We need to enjoy the rewards and use them to motivate ourselves to strive for even more.

So, let's get started on this journey of pursuing a life that matters and enjoy the discovery of what it means to live life well.

Part One

Get Ready!
What Is a Life
that Counts?

Chapter One

What Drives Your Life?

You have made my days a mere handbreadth;
the span of my years is as nothing before you.
Each man's life is but a breath.
PSALM 39:5

*E*mma's navy Suburban was fourth in the carpool line to pick up her third-grade son. He had a doctor's appointment across town in 20 minutes. Her eight-month-old was asleep in her car seat, and Emma had arranged for her five-year-old daughter to go home with a friend after preschool.

Everything was working like clockwork as Emma anxiously awaited her son's smiling face. A few minutes later, after calling his number several times without a response and being asked to pull up out of the way of the other cars, Emma was churning with anger. *Where in the world could he be? Why didn't he hear his carpool number? I don't have time to wait for him!*

Suddenly he appeared, a grin from cheek to cheek, arms overloaded as he juggled the class hamster cage, a big bag of food and supplies, and his backpack. His arms were so full he looked like he could fall over. Once he saw his mom, he naively exclaimed, "Mommy, my name got drawn to take home Hermie the hamster for the night!" His moment of celebration was short-lived, ended by the explosion of anger that erupted from his mother.

"David, what did I tell you this morning when I let you off?" she asked, without giving him time to answer. "I told you we would have a tight schedule because you have an appointment with Dr. Geoffrey. Get in the car. Hand me that thing!"

Between commands, eight-month-old Lilly woke up and started crying.

"Just get in the car, David." Emma slammed the doors after jamming the hamster cage and supplies in the backseat and David and backpack beside the hamster. She tore down the road, her tirade of disappointment in David rising over Lilly's screams. Emma was driving so fast and was so determined to make the appointment that she couldn't even see what was going on in the lives of the people she loved most. She didn't have time to think; she could only react, go, keep moving. She thought the only thing wrong was that she would be five minutes late. That and the question of what to do with a hamster while they were inside the doctor's office. She had no idea what was really wrong with her life.

It turned out the doctor was running late too, and Emma found time to regroup with David and Lilly. She told David she was sorry for getting so angry at him. They were able to go back out to the car and put Hermie in a safer place, carefully cracking each window. When they finally got in to see the doctor, Emma balanced Lilly, Lilly's bottle, and her own discontented disposition, while trying to take in everything the doctor was saying about David's asthma treatment. She scribbled a few notes with her left hand and prayed she'd be able to read them later.

After an hour and a half, Emma left the doctor's office and drove straight to her friend's house to pick up five-year-old Molly. Apologizing profusely for being late, she added Molly and Molly's just-finished art project to the Suburban and plunged ahead. It would be impossible to make dinner now, so she called from her cell phone and ordered pizza delivery.

At home, she cut up a few raw vegetables and set the pizza out for her family. By dinnertime her husband, Jim, was home, and he took over feeding Lilly while Emma ran back to change clothes, freshen her makeup, grab her things, and rush out to a women's event where she was hosting a table. She could feel a headache coming on, so she grabbed two aspirin, then quickly kissed everyone good-bye. She never noticed that Lilly's sticky fingers left her with a big smudge of cereal on the back of her dress.

No sooner had she gotten out the door than the cell phone rang. It was Jim, who didn't know what time to put the kids to bed. "Does David need a bath tonight?"

Having answered all Jim's questions, Emma pulled up to the church. The phone rang again. This time it was her best friend, Jane. Jane's boyfriend had just broken up with her, and she was distraught, calling to say that she couldn't pull it together enough to come to the dinner that night. She begged Emma to come by afterward; she desperately needed to talk.

Emma was concerned for her friend but also realized that Jane had forgotten she was to bring fresh flowers for the vases decorating the table. Jane was so upset that Emma couldn't ask about it, so she pulled out of her parking space and drove to the nearest grocery store, comforting Jane on the phone all the while. She arrived at the store and was dismayed to discover that the only available flowers were wilted carnations. She bought them anyway and rushed back to the church.

The event started five minutes later, and Emma felt like a fool reaching over the seated guests to place flowers in the vases. She looked around and sensed that every other table was more beautifully decorated than hers. She felt humiliated that she wasn't ready on time, and worse, as she reached to place the last flower, a woman sitting nearby noticed the white cereal smudge across her back and pointed it out to the whole table.

Emma quietly sat down, letting the back of the chair hide her smudge. She made an excuse for Jane and took full responsibility for being so scatterbrained that the table wasn't ready. She graciously led the table discussion and prayer, hiding her insecurity and exhaustion from everyone. It took her an hour to finish cleaning up after the event was over.

There was nothing Emma wanted more than to go home, go to bed, and forget this day, but she couldn't get Jane off her mind. First of all, she was mad at her for dumping on her at the last minute, but at the same time she felt sorry for Jane. It was 11 P.M., but she rushed right over to Jane's house and stayed until midnight, when she guiltily excused herself. She went home, left everything in the car, and fell into bed.

What's wrong with Emma's life? Does her life resemble yours? Maybe you don't have children at home or you're not married. Maybe you're a single mom or you're retired. But can you identify with Emma? Are the activities different but the scattered life the same? Are you very busy but feel you are letting everyone down? Maybe you can't remember the last meaningful moment you've shared with someone else, but you know you have a million things to get done. You can't remember the last time you had a totally guilt-free day, but you just keep pressing ahead, hoping that tomorrow will be different.

GOD CALLS YOU TO LIVE A LIFE THAT COUNTS

"Be very careful, then, how you live—not as unwise but as wise, making the most of every opportunity, because the days are evil" (Ephesians 5:15-16).

If Emma had read these verses right before she went to bed that night, they might have been the last straw for her. She might have curled up in a ball and faced the fact that she was just a big failure at living. She might have decided to give it all up, thinking, *What's the use anyway? I've got one more demand on my overly complicated life.*

But God's Word doesn't do that to us. It is sharper than a two-edged sword piercing the soul (Hebrews 4:12). Ephesians 5:15-16 is Emma's true liberation, for from this passage Emma can learn to find real excitement about the life she is living. If Emma will take time to stop and think about her life, she may find her life choices are causing her to miss important opportunities. She could discover how to live in a way that would make a big difference in the overall scheme of things.

You see, God wants Emma to live a life that counts, a life full of meaning and purpose. God wants to invite you to live a life that counts too. Our time here on earth is short compared to the time we will live eternally, but our first steps toward eternity begin the day we are born.

The apostle Paul decided that for him "to live is Christ" (Philippians 1:21). From that one decision he made many other decisions that brought peace and joy to his life on earth. Too many of us don't decide how we are going to live—life just happens. It's almost as if a job, a relationship, or a duty becomes your life. Living a life that matters involves being sure you are living a meaningful life. It requires making solid choices about how to live your life, rather than just letting life happen to you.

The problem with Emma's life is that she is so busy doing the things she needs to do every day, she doesn't have time to make changes. She may spend her next 10 years simply responding to what is asked and demanded of her without taking time to figure out what makes a life meaningful. Isn't it meaningful to take care of three young children, comfort a friend, and work at a church event? Emma doesn't stop to think about it, but deep down she sure does hope she's living a life that matters. What a sad reality she might wake up to if she discovered all the effort she put into her life didn't really count for much. She would get discouraged. Wouldn't you?

How Do You Know If You're Living a Life that Matters?

If there is some ingredient missing from Emma's life, she would like to know what it is. She is doing the best she can, and the last thing she needs is to have someone tell her there is something more she needs to add if she really wants to have a meaningful life.

It's not that Emma needs to add things to her life to make it count. In reality she needs to stop doing some things and rearrange other areas. In fact, that is what I found I needed to do in my own life to sense the fulfillment and assurance of the meaning I sought. I had to stop and ask myself some bold questions in order to get somewhere in the life I was living. I needed to get in touch with why and how God created me to find the right perspective on living a life that counts for Him.

Bold Questions

Ask yourself these bold questions to consider whether your life is in need of a transformation:

1. When you think of your relationship with God, do you feel guilty or wrong? Emma can never do enough for God. She loves Him and she knows He loves her, but she also feels He must be just as disappointed in her as are her parents, best friend, husband, and everyone else. But since He's not in her face, she doesn't think about it as much.

2. Are you afraid to yield your life to God's plan because He may have more for you to do than you are already doing now? One reason Emma doesn't slow down for God is she's trying to manage her already-packed life. If she were to slow down, God might give her something else to add to her list of things to do.

3. When you look at your calendar, checkbook, and daily experiences, do they seem like heavy burdens to bear? Emma's husband is great with the checkbook, so Emma doesn't worry there, but the calendar and daily experiences are definitely heavy, heavy burdens. She feels like a failure for thinking so.

4. Do you have relationships that deplete you? Do you think you might feel a bit depleted with a best friend like Jane? Emma believes it is her own failures that prevent her from giving Jane what she needs.

5. Do you ignore your bodily signals for rest, good nutrition, and exercise? Rest and exercise are down the drain in Emma's life. Nutrition does get met, but how good is it when at least three times a week your only vegetables are french fries?

6. Are you in financial bondage? Actually, Emma is not in financial bondage. She is very disciplined in this area of her life and so is her husband. She doesn't realize how blessed she is.

7. Do you sense God's disappointment in the way you live your life? Emma couldn't even imagine God being delighted in her. That seems so far from what a relationship between a sinful woman and a Holy God is all about.

God wants you to be able to answer no to every one of these questions. He doesn't want your life to be a burden. He wants you to be living a life that matters. He doesn't say that living a life that matters won't mean hard work and discipline. But all the hard work and discipline will have a specific purpose and bring deep meaning to your life. If Emma were living a life that matters, she could be looking forward to the breaking of each new day, rather than dreading what catastrophes it will hold.

Madge is a retired schoolteacher. She taught fourth grade for 35 years. When she retired five years ago, she went into a severe depression and found she no longer knew how to live her life. For so many years each day was determined for her by curriculum, school policies, and the calendar.

Suddenly, she was dropped into an unfamiliar world. It dawned on her that she had never developed the art of "hanging out" with friends during her years of working. She had friends, but she saw them at church, at school, and at social functions, not in day-to-day living.

When she told her doctor what was happening, she asked for a little time before she agreed to go on the antidepressant the doctor suggested. Instead, she went to see a counselor. The counselor became a sort of coach and simply taught Madge how to match God's priorities, her new life circumstances, and her personal interests to a life that was worth living. Eventually Madge could answer no, on most days, to every one of the bold questions asked above. She made important decisions about her life that brought true joy in living.

Characteristics of a Life that Matters

1. You feel loved and accepted by God. Being retired gave Madge many more opportunities to build her love relationship with God. Because she was not constrained by her job any longer, she had time to read Christian books, attend retreats, and go to a regular Bible study. All of these experiences increased her sense of how much God loves and accepts her.

2. You trust God's wisdom for your life. Madge discovered that God must have more life for her to live, since He had blessed her with health beyond her working years. Her husband had died before he had a chance to retire. Madge accepted her life as a gift from God with meaning and purpose. She began to see how much God could use her when she joined the intercessory prayer ministry at her church.

3. Your life—calendar, checkbook, experiences—reflects your priority of relationship with God and loving others. Even on a limited income, Madge didn't face financial worries. She learned how to depend on God for wisdom and guidance with her finances, her calendar, and the rest of her life.

4. You know how to deal with relationships that drain your energy, and you set proper boundaries. Madge didn't have a problem with draining relationships, but she had no meaningful relationships built into her life. Madge made an effort to build a tight support network of women she could count on to share her deepest fears and struggles.

5. You take care of your physical energy needs. One of the best decisions Madge made to fight her depression and contribute to a continued healthy life was to start an exercise program at the local YMCA She swims fours days a week and unexpectedly found a friend there too.

6. You live in financial freedom. Madge gained financial freedom through her school's excellent pension plan. She also realized that God helped her live off of what she had and saw her money as a gift from God. She determined not to use it selfishly.

7. You sense God's pleasure with you. In the end, Madge would say, "God is pleased with my perspective on life and how I am living." She still gossips and complains a little too much. She gets worried from time to time, and she isn't sinless. But she does know that she is walking in the general direction in which God is calling her. She wants to walk with Him more and more each day.

We are all aware of the kind of life that counts when it comes to the world's perspective. If you can make a lot of money, look attractive, be invited to join certain clubs, have political power, or have influence over a lot of people, you feel your life is important. But what kind of life does God honor?

In Hebrews 11 we learn that the ancients (biblical characters of history) were commended for their faith. Living a life that counts according to God's Word involves, among other things, not participating in gossip or slander, being sexually moral, sharing His love with other people, using our spiritual gifts, loving our families, and more. But all of these godly actions proceed through faith. What would God commend you for about your faith?

By faith Abel offered the pleasing sacrifice.

By faith Enoch was taken from this life without experiencing death.

By faith Noah built an ark.

By faith Abraham became the father of a nation through a barren, elderly wife.

By faith Isaac blessed Jacob.

By faith Jacob worshiped God.

By faith Joseph prophesied about the coming exodus.

By faith Moses' parents hid him from Pharaoh.

By faith Moses led the children of Israel to the Promised Land.

By faith the Israelites passed through the Red Sea.

By faith Rahab hid the spies and was not killed when the walls of Jericho fell.

By faith kings were conquered, justice was administered, promises were received, lions' mouths were shut, fires were put out, wars were won.

Because of their faith many were tortured, beaten, and killed.

By faith Deborah ignored the voices that promised her what she could be and listened to the Voice that called her by name and promised her nothing except that which she really needed.

How would God complete this sentence about you? "By faith, _____ (your name) _____."

A life that matters is a life of faith. You won't necessarily see how much a person's life counts by how many recordings he sells or how high she ranks in the popularity profile. In God's accounting system, a life that counts may be obscure to the world. It may not receive attention from anyone or be recognized as anything special by our culture's standards. But a life of faith is a life that counts.

Do You Want to Live a Life that Counts?

The answer to that question seems obvious, doesn't it? Everyone wants to live a life that counts. I'm sure of that. But too many of us are unwilling to give up what seems comfortable in order to make our lives count. We're afraid of change. We are afraid to abandon what has worked for us for years (even if it's no longer working). What would make it worth it for you to change? God motivates us with promises of rich rewards, which we'll look at in the next chapter.

Journal Exercise

1. How would I be willing to make major adjustments in my life if I felt God leading me to make them?
2. Am I willing to think outside of the box to discover what I can really do with my life? How?
3. Do I see my life as a gift to me that has many choices I can make about how to live it? Why or why not?
4. What I like most about my life right now is . . .
5. What I think God is most pleased with about my life right now is . . .
6. The part of my life that I am most resistant to change is . . .
7. The way I would describe my dream life is . . .

Goal for the Week

Imagine what it would be like if you could honestly answer no to the seven bold questions:

1. When you think of your relationship with God, do you feel guilty or wrong?
2. Are you afraid to yield your life to God's plan because He may have more for you to do than you are already doing now?
3. When you look at your calendar, checkbook, and daily experiences, do they seem like heavy burdens to bear?
4. Do you have relationships that deplete you?
5. Do you ignore your bodily signals for rest, good nutrition, and exercise?
6. Are you in financial bondage?
7. Do you sense God's disappointment in the way you live your life?

Chapter Two

The Kind of Life God Rewards

But our citizenship is in heaven. And we eagerly await a
Savior from there, the Lord Jesus Christ.
PHILIPPIANS 3:20

*E*xcept for the occasional crisis that knocks her for a loop, Elizabeth is one of the happiest people you would ever meet. She's 37, single, and expecting to become vice president of her company by next year. She has plenty of money, lots of friends, is very active at her church, and is never at a loss for exciting and wonderful things to do and people to meet. However, she says that she would give up all of the perks of being a businesswoman in a minute if she could just find the right man. In the meantime, though, she feels she is living life to the fullest.

Elizabeth arranged for a "Making Over Your Life" seminar for her church singles' group. It was a one-day event in which the speaker focused on the priorities we need to think about as we live our everyday lives. If there was one thing the single women she met at church seemed to lack, it was focus. She hoped to help them fix up their lives by establishing priorities in keeping with God's Word, as she herself had done. The funny thing was, when she actually sat down and listened to the speaker, she discovered her own important and powerful life needed improvement. Initially she thought she was doing just fine, but when she was challenged to examine her life from God's priorities, she changed her mind.

The speaker began by talking about the judgment seat of Christ (also known as the *bema* seat) mentioned in 2 Corinthians 5:10. He began by telling a fictional story of a man experiencing that judgment. The man described had been quite successful with the things of the world. He had always felt blessed by God because of all the exciting things he got to do and wonderful places he was able to go.

When the man stood at the judgment seat, however, evaluations were made on a whole new system of measurement. Instead of success resting on the amount of money made in life, success depended on the amount of money donated to the poor. Rewards were not given for the number of hours dedicated to a job, but rather for how many people one witnessed to about Christ while on the job. The man who had always been proud of himself and his accomplishments now felt small and sad and disappointed that he had used his lifetime, talents, money, and energy to focus on the wrong things. Elizabeth totally identified with this man.

In contrast to Elizabeth, the apostle Paul was a person with complete confidence in the way he lived his life. In 2 Timothy 4:7-8 he boldly states, "I have fought the good fight, I have finished the race, I have kept the faith. Now there is in store for me the crown of righteousness, which the Lord, the righteous Judge, will award to me on that day—and not only to me, but also to all who have longed for his appearing."

Paul was absolutely convinced that he had lived a life that mattered. He recognized the power of the Holy Spirit enabling him to heal, preach, love, debate, build tents, and meet people—indeed, helping in every aspect of his life. He had no idea that his inspired writings would fill up so many pages of the New Testament and be used to encourage and motivate churches for centuries to follow Christ. In other words, he didn't really know the full extent of the impact of his life lived for Christ. Still, he felt complete confidence in the life he chose to live and looked forward to the day when he would experience the joy of receiving the promised rewards for a life well lived.

You might think a preacher, a missionary like Paul, or a women's Bible study leader would have good reason to feel confident. But not someone like you, "just an ordinary person." Not true, according to Paul. He says Jesus is longing to hand out rewards on Judgment Day. He is waiting to give these rewards to everyone who longs for His coming. He wants to reward everyone who has a driving passion to please Him. That's the amazing thing about living a life that counts: We can all live one.

If you go to Nashville and look around, you will find plenty of talented musicians who feel like complete nobodies. God may have given them impressive voices and keen minds for blending moving lyrics with harmonies and melodies, but they never get noticed. Why? One reason is there are so many more talented songwriters and musicians who want to earn a living with music than there are consumers and record companies giving out contracts. Only a very few who strive for best-selling albums actually make the cut. Not so with living a life that counts: Each of us is equally eligible. Each of us can receive the reward Paul was so sure was his.

Don't you want to feel the same way as Paul about the way you live your life? Don't you want that same confidence? You can have it. The secret to being confident that you live a life that counts is to live a life focused on Jesus Christ. As mentioned previously, Paul said that when it came right down to it, "to live is Christ" (Philippians 1:21). What did Paul mean by that?

Paul's driving motivation was to please Jesus Christ. His prominent focus and passion was to live a life that was a pleasing sacrifice (see Romans 12:1). He lived his life in such a way that he would bring pleasure to God.

My son is going to make a great husband someday. He has studied me and found the thing that brings great pleasure to my heart: He brings me chocolate! Often after chocolate is handed out at school as a reward or treat, he presents me with a melted, battered candy bar when I pick him up at the end of the day. Rather than eating his prize, he slips it into his pocket so he can present it to me as a pleasing sacrifice. There is no chocolate in the world that tastes better than a melted, dirty Hershey's Kiss saved for you by your son. It literally brings tears to my eyes to realize the sacrifice and care that goes into his gift.

Don't you think in time I want to reward a son like that? I don't take him right out at that moment to buy a game or whatever item he wants. That would diminish his gift. But his action registers in my positive feelings of motherhood. It is going to be rewarded eventually. Of course, he also gets the immediate reward of having a mom in a very happy mood.

God Is Into Rewards

Trying to earn rewards from God may not seem right to you. Aren't you supposed to please God because He loves you? Isn't that reward enough? Not when you are the God who is filled with love and delight in your children. In fact, Hebrews 11:6 says, "Without faith it is impossible to please God, because anyone who comes to him must believe that he exists and *that he rewards those who earnestly seek him*" (emphasis mine). God doesn't want you to be in it only for the reward, but He does want you to have faith that He is a God who rewards. There's a big difference.

When you do it for the reward, you will stop doing it if you don't get a reward. Your heart isn't in it. God rewards, but He only rewards those whose hearts are right. He rewards those who seek Him with all their hearts. (See Matthew 6:33.)

The parable of the shrewd manager (Luke 16) has always been a passage that bothered me because I had a hard time understanding what Jesus was getting at by saying, "The people of this world are more shrewd in dealing with their own kind than are the people of the light" (v. 8). The parable tells of a manager of an estate who was wasting his master's resources. The master was angry and told the manager he was about to be fired. When the manager was closing up the accounts, he made canny deals with the people who owed his master. He told them to change their bills to a lesser amount than they actually owed. The manager did this because he was thinking of his future. He was hoping that these debtors would reward him in the future for what he had done. When the master found out about his manager's shenanigans, he praised him.

On the surface, it seems the manager has no character qualities we should imitate. But Jesus uses the story to tell us something. There was something about how this manager lived his life that Jesus wants you and me to emulate.

Now, what could it be? Are we being told to misuse our earthly master's wealth? No. Should we be cheating, lying, and stealing? No, that is ruled out in other scriptures. Then what is it? Why did the master commend his manager? He was shrewd. It's as if the master was saying, "I've got to hand it to you. I didn't see that one coming when I told you to close the accounts. But you were perceptive, because you closed the accounts in such a way that you helped yourself for your future."

God wants us to be shrewd managers of our lives. We shouldn't be looking only at our present accounts, when our statements come quarterly. He wants us to live our lives understanding that how we live now will make a difference in the future, indeed for eternity.

The years that we are given to live on this round blue sphere have a deeper purpose. People who live lives that count acknowledge that reality and think not only of what happens on earth, but how it affects eternity. We don't know everything about heaven, yet the Bible lets us in on a few secrets, so we should pay attention to them. For instance, a number of Scripture's references to heaven involve crowns.

I have never worn a crown on earth. I was a member of the homecoming court in high school and college, but I was never the queen. I remember wanting a crown to hold my veil for my wedding dress, but to cut costs I borrowed my sister's crown-less veil instead. Though I often wanted to wear a crown, I've been denied that possibility. Denied a crown on earth, I'm even more amazed that God wants to give me one in heaven.

In a beauty pageant only the winner wears the real crown. That's what makes it special: Only one can receive it. But God has an overabundance of crowns. Every saint can have one. There are certain behaviors He is looking for when He hands them out. He doesn't give crowns for nothing. He gives them to the faithful.

A vision of heaven in Revelation 4:10-11 gives a glimpse of what our crowns will mean to us. "The twenty-four elders fall down before him who sits on the throne, and worship him who lives for ever and ever. They lay their crowns before the throne and say: 'You are worthy, our Lord and God, to receive glory and honor and power, for you created all things, and by your will they were created and have their being.' "

You see, these crowns are not only our rewards but also a means of worshipping God. How completely different from the crowns I have wanted to wear on earth.

Crowns, Crowns, and More Crowns

Salvation is by faith and is a free gift to all who believe in the name of Jesus Christ. Crowns are rewards that Jesus bestows on His followers for the way they lived on earth. Yet our greatest reward is a restored relationship with Jesus Christ.

Genesis 15:1 states, "After this, the word of the LORD came to Abram in a vision: 'Do not be afraid, Abram. I am your shield, your very great reward.' " Indeed, Jesus Christ is our very great reward! We are rewarded in full, so why would we seek a greater reward? I encourage you to be bold and diligent with your life to gather rewards from Jesus so that one day you and I, along with the 24 elders, will be able to lay them at the feet of Jesus. What a reward to reward the Rewarder.

With my fixation on crowns, I've done a little study of the kinds of crowns Jesus gives and what they mean. If I'm going to be a shrewd manager of what my Master has entrusted to me, I've got to do my research. Let's look at the first of five different crowns found in Scripture.

The incorruptible crown (1 Corinthians 9:25). Olympic athletes must devote countless hours to training and preparation in order to receive a crown (medal, reward). They give up desserts, time with families, ordinary lives, comfort, and safety. After they have put time, talents, and abilities into reaching their goals, a few may even win medals, but their "crowns" will not last forever. Within a short time, a world record may fall to a competitor.

Every reward a person could seek is corruptible . . . unless (and here's the catch) you do it for the Lord. "Whatever you do, work at it with all your heart, as working for the Lord, not for men, since you know that you will receive an inheritance from the Lord as a reward. It is the Lord Christ you are serving" (Colossians 3:23-24).

This incorruptible crown is given as a reward to those who serve on this earth as if they are serving the Lord. Why am I writing this book? Am I trying to get on the bestseller list? Am I after a publishing industry award? Do I want fame, popularity, money? Why am I spending the time away from my family, typing away on my computer, putting down my thoughts and ideas? Unless I am writing this book to serve God out of my love for Him and the people He loves, all my hard work won't last. These hours of dedication and service may make a difference in someone else's life, but it will mean nothing for me in eternity if I don't give with the right motive.

Sometimes I cringe to think of all the things going on in the name of Jesus that are not for Him, in Him, or through Him at all. They will burn up. Everything you do to serve the Lord with the right motives will last for eternity.

When my children were small, I regularly received artwork, projects, and crafts from almost every activity they attended—church, preschool, choir, missions organizations, and Indian Guides and Princesses. It became overwhelming because I couldn't throw them away. I displayed some and put the others on top of the refrigerator. When they were piled so high that they reached the ceiling, I had to do something. When the kids were out of the house or down for a nap, I went through that large pile. I threw away everything I could bear to discard, but I still kept a lot—things that reminded me uniquely of them. I still have those projects stashed in my garage. Everything made by my children was corruptible, doomed for the trash can someday. Still, some of it was saved; I couldn't bear to throw it away.

Jesus feels the same about our little projects. In reality they are all corruptible. But some of our deeds are very special, and the projects we complete in His strength and for His glory could never be thrown away. They reveal that we understand Him and that we are actually grasping His monumental love for us. They will never be sent to the refuse pile but will be cherished for eternity.

The crown of rejoicing (1 Thessalonians 2:19). This crown is known as the soul-winners crown. Paul spoke of the salvation of those in Thessalonica who were saved by his ministry as his own crown.

There is nothing like bringing others into the kingdom of God. Some people have the gift of evangelism and, therefore, enjoy this unique experience quite often. Each of us has opportunities to share God's Word, peace, and truth. Introducing someone to a personal relationship with God is a blessed experience.

Personally, I don't have a long list of converts, but I have been blessed to be a part of the rebirth of many. One that stands out was the salvation of my own daughter. She was only five, so though I prayed for her salvation, I wasn't expecting it to happen at such a young age. I was practicing the Vacation Bible School story I would be teaching the next week. She sat there, my only attendant, and listened to my words. When I finished, she said she wanted to pray to accept Jesus as her Savior. I was a little surprised. I didn't want it to happen then because we weren't in town with her father. I willingly prayed with her but secretly doubted that she had meant it. She went right out of the room and started telling everyone what she had just done. One of her uncles told her to call her daddy and tell him because he would be very proud. Even though I didn't think it was the right time and I wasn't planning on evangelizing my daughter, she came to Christ. About four years later, she led her brother to Christ.

The crown of righteousness (2 Timothy 4:8). This can also be called the crown of watchfulness. Paul knew that crown was waiting for him, polished and bright. The crown of righteousness is granted to those who long for, watch for, and eagerly await Christ's appearance. There's a real balancing act for Christians as they live on earth as citizens of earthly kingdoms, while recognizing that in the future the heavenly kingdom will be revealed. Christians are encouraged to live lives that are worthy of this heavenly kingdom.

In 2 Peter 3:11-14 we are encouraged to live holy, godly lives, spotless, blameless, and at peace as we wait. The waiting is both passive and

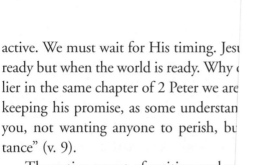 

active. We must wait for His timing. Jes~~~ ready but when the world is ready. Why ~ lier in the same chapter of 2 Peter we are keeping his promise, as some understan you, not wanting anyone to perish, bu tance" (v. 9).

The active aspect of waiting and w~~~~~~~ ~~~~~ ~~~ ~ godly, holy, blameless, spotless, and peaceful life. The motivation for this kind of life is a steadfast belief that the things of this world are not all there is. You can say no to the ungodly, unholy, shameful, dirty, fretful life options that are offered you. If you say no because you are eager for God's appearance, you will receive a reward—the crown of righteousness.

The crown of life (Revelation 2:10; James 1:12). Some call this the martyr's crown. If you read the book of Revelation, you can ascertain that those who have given their lives for the sake of the gospel are very special to God. But you could also interpret this as a reward given to all who suffer in Christ.

There is a reward in this life for suffering in Christ. I've counseled many who have suffered unfair and unprecedented hardships; they wouldn't exchange their suffering if it meant never feeling the comfort of God. Whether you believe this crown is awarded only to those who are literally martyred for their faith, or for all who suffer in other ways because of their faith, it is clear there is a reward waiting in heaven for those who suffer.

The crown of glory (1 Peter 5:4). This crown is often referred to as the shepherd's crown. It is reserved for those who fulfill the task of shepherding the flock in the absence of the Chief Shepherd. Those shepherds who lead the flock to spiritual water, food, and shelter will be rewarded in a special way.

There is nothing more important than knowing the Scriptures to cultivate your personal relationship with God. You are rewarded for our spiritual food with the flock. When you put your efforts nowing, doing, and teaching God's Word, you are rewarded with crown of glory.

In Ezra 7:10 we read, "For Ezra had devoted himself to the study and observance of the Law of the Lord, and to teaching its decrees and laws in Israel." We must approach God's Word in this same order. It is because I have devoted myself to studying God's Word and then obeying it, that I am granted the privilege of teaching you what I have learned. So many would like the job of shepherding the flock, telling others what to do. But a shepherd worthy of the crown of glory has lived the Word before teaching it.

Eliza E. Hewitt (1851-1920) wrote the hymn "Will There Be Any Stars in My Crown?" The hymn writer assumes that stars in the crown are representations of people won to Christ. The hymn leads us to consider why we would desire stars in our crowns and helps us imagine how we might feel on that day when the rewards will be delivered.

Will There Be Any Stars in My Crown?
I am thinking today of that beautiful land
I shall reach when the sun goeth down;
When through wonderful grace by my Savior I stand,
Will there be any stars in my crown?
Refrain: *Will there be any stars, any stars in my crown*
when at evening the sun goeth down?
When I wake with the blessed in the mansions of rest
Will there be any stars in my crown?
In the strength of the Lord let me labor and pray,
Let me watch as a winner of souls,
That bright stars may be mine in the glorious day,
When His praise like the sea billow rolls.
O what joy it will be when His face I behold,
Living gems at his feet to lay down!
It would sweeten my bliss in the city of gold,
Should there be any stars in my crown.

Journal Exercise

How many of the five crowns are waiting for you?
1. The Incorruptible Crown
   What do you do solely to glorify God?
2. The Crown of Rejoicing
   Name the people you have personally led to salvation in Christ.
3. The Crown of Righteousness
   List the ways that your life reveals your focus on Christ's return.
   Are you living in a way that is:
   godly?
   holy?
   blameless?
   spotless?
   peaceful?
4. The Crown of Life
   In what areas have you suffered for Christ?
5. The Crown of Glory
   How are you helping others follow God?

Goal for the Week

Each time you look into the clouds, imagine Christ bursting through them to take you to heaven.

Chapter Three

A Picture of a Life that Counts

Since, then, you have been raised with Christ,
set your hearts on things above,
where Christ is seated at the right hand of God.
Set your minds on things above, not on earthly things.
COLOSSIANS 3:1-2

I wish that we could all gather around the table and play a Christian board game called Generosity.[1] My husband picked it up at a Christian bookstore and our kids enjoyed playing it. It stands out in stark contrast to games like Monopoly, Mall Madness, Life, and other board games we have also enjoyed as a family, as it illustrates the same heavenly principles that you are exploring as you seek to pursue a life that matters.

At the beginning of the game each player is assigned a vocation such as missionary, doctor, lawyer, secretary, and so forth. Incomes are consistent with those of the actual vocations. The missionary, for example, will make much less money than the doctor. Winning isn't based on the amount of money made in a lifetime, but how much money a player puts into a heavenly treasure chest.

Surprisingly, even if someone makes five times another person's income, both players end up with equal opportunities to contribute to the heavenly treasure chest. You can only put money into the treasure chest if you have the right attitude, which is determined by drawing a card. Throughout the game you have numerous opportunities to give to others; every penny you give goes into your own heavenly treasure chest.

After all the players have made it to heaven, there is a "day of reckoning," when the players count the money in their heavenly treasure chests. The winner is the one who has the most invested in his or her treasure chest; all the rest of their belongings and holdings are valueless. This game is a direct parallel to real life. The way we choose to spend our time and money will bring rewards at the day of reckoning.

The Epistles of Paul offer a number of challenges and encouragement to live lives worthy of reward. *Why so many?* I have wondered. Paul revealed something about his spiritual life in 2 Corinthians 12 that shows me he knew what he was talking about. In verses 8-9 Paul described his thorn in the flesh, which he begged God to remove, though God did not. God explained to Paul that His grace was made perfect in his (Paul's) weakness. But earlier, in verse 7, Paul says that his thorn helped to keep him humble.

You see, Paul had been granted a unique and special privilege. He actually experienced paradise. He wasn't sure if it was a vision, or if he actually was in heaven, but he did write about having heard "inexpressible things, things that man is not permitted to tell" (2 Corinthians 12:4).

Though Jesus taught us to be watchful, and the other biblical writers echo this thought, Paul gives us compelling and insistent direction to consider eternity while living on earth. He certainly didn't break God's command not to speak of anything that he was not permitted to tell us. He was unable to tell us everything, but he did insist that a life lived well will be rewarded in heaven.

THERE ARE REWARDS

In Revelation 22:12 Jesus says He is coming for us and that His reward is with Him. In Matthew 16:27, Jesus says that He is coming in His Father's glory with His angels to reward each person according to what he has done. Throughout the Old and New Testaments, God promises us rewards. Romans 14:12, Romans 2:6 and 16, Proverbs 24:12, Isaiah 40:10, and Psalm 62:12 provide examples of this promise. How does this promise of reward apply to our lives today? We all know that modern life offers a great deal to keep us busy. No matter who you are, what your situation, or where you live, our fast-paced culture can allow you to fill your days with activities from morning till night. Recognize that some of the things that you do will be rewarded in heaven, but many of the things you do will be meaningless by next week.

I am working on this chapter in the midst of the busiest time of all—Christmas. Parties and special events crowd the calendar throughout the month of December. I've finished my decorating, but I've got shopping, baking, wrapping, and card writing, all waiting to be crossed off my list. I ask myself, "Why do I do so much at Christmas?" "Why do I wipe myself out?" "What is the purpose?"

Jesus wants me to ask that same question, not just at Christmas, but every day of my life. Whether I'm paying attention to my life or not, Jesus is. He is inside of me, encouraging me to think of eternal things. He doesn't want me just living for today or living for Christmas Day, but living for eternity. Paul understood that so well.

Remember that we will all appear before the judgment (*bema*) seat of Christ to receive rewards for how we lived on earth (2 Corinthians 5:10). This is not the great white throne judgment mentioned in Revelation 20:11. All Christians will escape that judgment because our names are written in the Book of Life. The judgment that Paul writes about is something altogether different. It is only for believers. It is referred to as the *bema* seat because *bema* is the Greek word for *judgment*.

The *bema* seat was the raised platform used to award prizes in the Grecian games, the place where judges rewarded those who ran the fastest race. Likewise, the judgment seat of Christ will be the place where Jesus rewards those who have used their lifetimes on earth to honor and glorify Him. Only the fastest and the best stood before the judgment seat at the Grecian games. God says that every believer will stand before His judgment seat.

At the Olympic games, judges use certain criteria to deliver rewards. Participants hire coaches and assistants who are well aware of the criteria judges use to determine which athlete is best. This is especially important in competitions where the time clock does not determine the best performance. Knowing the standards ahead of time, athletes put all their efforts into fulfilling judges' expectations.

Jesus is our Judge, the One who rewards each of us for a life lived well. He is not a subjective judge; He spells out His criteria for us. His Word describes the characteristics necessary to a life that counts. Being rewarded by Jesus is not an elusive ideal. Remember the apostle Paul's confidence as he came to the end of his life. He was eager to receive the rewards promised to him. Jesus wants you and me to discover that same kind of confidence in our lives.

For What Does Jesus Grant Rewards?

Jesus gives us a clear picture of what He is looking for in our lives. Did you ever have a teacher who would throw a major question on the exam from the footnotes or some other obscure passage? Don't you hate it when a teacher tries to trip you up on a test, rather than giving you an opportunity to show how much you do know? Well, Jesus isn't trying to trip us up. He lays out His expectations in black and white.

Scripture describes seven areas of life that matter a great deal to Jesus. Some of these are reminiscent of the crowns discussed in the previous chapter.

1. Jesus gives heavenly rewards to those who use their financial resources for His kingdom (Matthew 6:19-21). Money is a key area of criticism directed toward the church. Some unchurched people complain that "they are always asking for money." If Christians were living according to God's principles, the church wouldn't need to ask for money; rather it would need to ask, "How can all this money be used to glorify God?"

I really don't envy the extremely wealthy, because they have difficult issues to work through. Yes, God has blessed the rich abundantly, but

He has also challenged them immensely. I know several people who've made millions of dollars and have been faithful to God with what He has entrusted to them. I admire them yet wonder if I would have been as faithful. The temptation to spend it only on myself and my wants is a powerful one.

Have you ever been given a lot of money and just blown it? I know I have. It may not have been millions, but I do regret not being more grateful and more resourceful with the money God has given me over my lifetime. Awareness of my overabundance may indicate that He has been giving me an opportunity to bless others rather than indulge myself. God notices how I spend His money. God will reward me in heaven for the way I have spent the resources entrusted to me on earth.

What kinds of investments do you make into your heavenly bank account? Are you managing your resources well enough that you are able to give to God's kingdom? Do you respond to the prompting of the Holy Spirit to give? (See 2 Corinthians 8:7.)

2. Jesus gives rewards for the spiritual disciplines we practice with the right motives (Matthew 5-8, 16-18; 1 Corinthians 9:17; 1 Corinthians 4:5). If your boss (or family, if you work at home) came to you and granted you a one-week vacation from what you regularly do, along with the resources to do whatever you wanted above all else, how would you spend that week? How do you suppose Jesus would spend a week on earth, if God didn't have anything else planned for Him to do? Don't you think He would want to spend it in solitude with God, perhaps on a mountain retreat?

I long to long for solitude with God the way Jesus did. He loved being with His disciples, nurturing their tender faith. He must have felt joy in healing the sick, bringing them closer to God's original design. He enjoyed a good theological debate. But, each time Jesus caught a little free time, guess where He went? He withdrew from people to spend time with God.

Too many of us live our time on earth without learning how to connect with God. Prayer, fasting, and Bible study are some of the spiritual disciplines that draw us closer to Him. Every moment spent in prayer, fasting, meditating on God's Word, worshiping, and celebrating God is rewarded both on earth and in heaven.

I've been reading and meditating on God's Word daily since I was 16 years old. I have missed a few days, and on even more days I did it without the right motive. But the years of spending quality time with God have made me more powerful spiritually, increasing my connection to God and deepening my spiritual insights. My time with Him has equipped me for helping others sense His leading in their lives. It has humbled me, strengthened me, comforted me, and guided me. I would not trade one moment I have spent in prayer, fasting, and reading the Word.

The impact on my spiritual life is not my only reward, though. I'll be rewarded in heaven as well. Even now, as I write to you with a heart that longs to see you living a life that matters, the results of the spiritual disciplines benefit me, they benefit you, and they are blessed and rewarded by God in heaven. Incredible, isn't it!

3. Jesus gives rewards for standing up for your faith (Matthew 5:11-12; Luke 6:22-23; Revelation 2:10; James 1:12). Paul proclaimed over and over that he was not ashamed of the gospel. Obviously some people were ashamed of the gospel, for they wanted to keep their relationship with God a secret. Most of the passages here refer to standing up for your faith to the point that you would die for it.

As a young child, I remember hearing a missionary tell a story about a girl who was around my age at the time. She was part of a church in a region of the world that was antagonistic to Christ. The missionary told how the police came to the church and started hauling people out. At the doorway to the church they placed a picture of Christ. They brought each parishioner to the picture of Christ and said, "If you spit on the face of Christ, you can go home. If not, we will kill you." Many people spat on that picture and walked away from the church. That 10-year-old girl, I was told, refused to spit on Christ and was martyred for her faith.

What I remember most about hearing that story was how I thought, *I'm sure that God would have forgiven her if she had spat on Jesus. He would know that in her heart she really didn't mean it.* Much later in my life, I finally understood the significance of that young girl's actions. Jesus has made a blood covenant with me, a promise that cannot be broken. Even if I do break my side of it, He will not break His. So, the little girl would not have been cast away from God if she had chosen to spit, but in her heart she would have suffered. When we don't keep our covenant with Jesus, it hurts.

I've got to admit, I don't plan, hope, or desire to be martyred for my faith, and I certainly would not want that for my loved ones. God doesn't want us to be martyred either, but if we are, and for those who have been, there awaits an important reward. Those martyrs are very dear and precious in the kingdom. Revelation 6:9-11 reveals how precious these saints are to God. God has them near His throne, and He listens lovingly to their cry for justice. He responds in care and concern for their suffering.

The majority of Christians who have lived these past two thousand years have done so without the threat of martyrdom. In America we can worship in freedom without fear of losing our lives. Still, Christians do feel threatened to share who they really are with a godless world. They may fear rejection or ridicule, or they may fear being a poor representation of Christ. However, Jesus rewards us for taking a stand for Him and not being ashamed of Him.

4. Jesus gives rewards for the way you treat others (Matthew 10:40-42; Luke 14:12-14; Hebrews 6:10; 1 Thessalonians 2:19-20; Mark 9:41; Luke 6:32-35). Here's where it really gets good. Jesus loves to see you living your life like He did. He longs to see you treating others well. If you give just one cup of water in the name of Jesus, you will be rewarded. There's a song lyric that reminds us, "You're the only Jesus some will ever see." That's one very important reason He rewards those who care for others. Jesus enlists us as helpers on the journey of meeting people's needs.

In Acts 10:4 we read that Cornelius was commended by a visiting angel for his prayer and gifts to the poor. "Your prayers and gifts to the poor have come up as a memorial offering before God."

I live in a city where beggars stand at intersections asking for help because of their difficult lives. Their signs claim that they are hungry and willing to work, or they are veterans, or they are just in need. I can see that they have been bruised and battered by life, yet people warn me that giving them money just perpetuates their struggles in life. Many panhandlers use the money to buy more drugs or alcohol, often the cause of their poverty. I don't want to give them money to make their problems worse, but I also don't want to drive by and communicate that I don't care for them at all. I prayed about this, and God inspired me to make care bags. I fill them with nonperishable items such as peanut butter crackers, candy, and bottled water. God cares for those poor people who stand at the intersections of my life, and He asks me to make a difference in theirs.

I heard a woman tell about her conversion experience, describing how she had been an alcoholic and drug addict, running from her family, God, and the law. After spending the night in jail, she hit bottom and cried out to God. She remembered the things she had been taught as a young child in church. She asked God if He would help her. When she got out of jail and the taxi let her out by her car that had been parked at her workplace, she noticed there was something on her windshield under the wiper. She looked at the other cars and saw their windshields were empty, so she assumed it was a parking ticket, just something else that had gone wrong in her life. When she lifted the wiper, she found a modern translation of the New Testament. She held it to her heart and started to cry, assured that God had answered her request for help. She began attending church and found a Christian 12-step meeting. Her life is now lived for Jesus.

When I heard her story, I thought about how different her life would have been had some person *not* put that Bible on her car. That person will never know how obedience to the Holy Spirit's prompting made such a dramatic difference in a woman's life, but Jesus does, and one day He will reward the obedient one.

5. Jesus gives rewards for dedicating everything you do to glorify God (Colossians 3:23-25; Romans 12:1). Glorify God in everything.

Does that include cleaning your toilets? Jesus rewards preachers, missionaries, and Bible study leaders, but He also rewards secretaries, computer programmers, doctors, lawyers, and stay-at-home moms based on the same criteria. His rewards depend on whether a person's actions grow from a desire to glorify Him.

It would be a lot easier if He had just said, "I'll reward everyone who surrenders their vocation to full-time Christian ministry." But that's not the basis of the reward. It is based on whether or not you have a heavenly mind-set as you perform your earthly vocation. Being a stay-at-home mom, maid, dental hygienist, teacher, financial broker, or architect won't disqualify you from the reward, but being a preacher won't automatically make you a shoo-in, either.

Jesus rewards us for living our day-to-day lives with the goal of pleasing Him. Jesus was the perfect example. He told us that He came to do what the Father was doing (John 5:19). It wasn't like He came to earth with a computer disk installed in His brain: On Tuesday you will raise a boy from the dead; Wednesday, you will call your disciples. Rather, it appears through the words He spoke that He waited and watched each day to discover the tasks the Father had for Him that day, and then He did them.

Oh, what an exciting, wonderful, fulfilling life I could live, if I learned the discipline of glorifying the Father!

6. Jesus gives rewards for keeping God's Word pure (2 John 7-8; Revelation 2–3). I love this one. I love God's Word. I love to study the Word in an applicational manner and teach others how to hear what God has to say to them personally about their own problems, situations, and life experiences.

Jesus commended the churches of Ephesus and Philadelphia for keeping His Word (Revelation 2–3).

God's Word is an amazing miracle. No other holy book in any religion can make the claims of God's Word. None can boast of the quality and consistency of the Old and New Testaments that make up our Bible. We can trust it to be the infallible Word of God that can guide and direct our relationship with Him.

7. Jesus gives rewards for being watchful for His return (2 Timothy 4:8; Luke 12:35-48; Mark 13:32-37). Jesus taught His disciples to watch for His return. Two thousand years later, we can see that His return wasn't even close to their lifetimes. Why would Jesus want them to be watchful? He wants every generation to be watchful for His return, because even if we do not live in a time when His return is imminent, we will spend our days with an eye on eternity.

How would you live if you knew for certain that Jesus would return in 10 years? What would you want Jesus to find you doing? Living with that question in your mind can lead you to focus your life on different priorities. It will help you reduce distractions and remain true to what He is calling you to do.

Journal Exercise

If you knew for sure that Jesus was returning for you six months from today, how would you want to be living? List activities or disciplines that you feel are important to Jesus that you have done in the past, or that you believe God wants you to be doing now.

Goal for the Week

Get ahead for next week. The journal exercise for chapter four involves taking inventory of how you spend your time during a one-week period. If you want to be prepared by the end of the chapter, start your inventory today. Look at pages 43-44 to receive instructions for the inventory.

Chapter Four

What Kind of Life Are You Living?

Our people must learn to devote themselves
to doing what is good, in order that they may provide
for daily necessities and not live unproductive lives.
TITUS 3:14

ere is where the proverbial rubber meets the road. It's time to make your passion for living a life that matters merge with your real, everyday, hour-by-hour, minute-by-minute life. We can agree it's important to live life well. We can desire the rewards that Jesus promises when we serve Him for the right reasons. We can determine to stop wasting our time, money, and effort on things that can be taken away from us. But if we don't take *action*, we will never live that life. Living a life that matters requires CHANGE!

After the release of my book in 1997, now called *A Woman's Search for Worth*,[1] some friends said they were unhappy that a test in the book revealed they had control issues. Brenda Mammel was one of those friends. I never realized how much God had done in her life as a result of that discovery until she wrote me a letter after she had climbed her first mountain, the Grand, one of the Grand Tetons in Wyoming. I had moved away from Brenda, but when she decided to train for and climb the Grand Tetons, she thought of me. She remembered that I had said

Jackson Hole, Wyoming, and the Grand Tetons were the most beautiful places I had ever seen. She wanted me to share in her enthusiasm, celebration, and prayer for the journey. After her climb she wrote:

> Well, as you know, according to your book I was a control freak. I must admit I didn't know I was until I read your book. Thanks for opening my eyes. Unfortunately, due to issues in my past [Brenda's dad was sick all throughout her childhood and died at age 38 when she was just turning seven], I had seen tragedy and because of this I began trying to control everything around me. Why? In order to protect myself from painful situations. This control let few people into my life and also led to my continual bartering with God. I assumed that since my father was so deathly ill all my childhood and since we had been so poor, God would give me what I wanted.
>
> When my kids came along that's when the wheeling and dealing began. "Now God, I've already had enough sickness and pain in my life. I've paid my dues. Please keep my kids safe and healthy." I would pray that prayer often. I lived in fear. Well, two years ago Jessica was diagnosed with Type I juvenile diabetes. I was broken—broken into a hundred pieces because I knew what this disease does to people. I see the results of the disease while working with patients who have called 911. [Brenda is a firefighter by profession.] I couldn't believe God didn't keep our deal. I came to Him pleading, trying to explain how I wasn't going to be able to handle this. I tried to tell Him I had already experienced enough. Instead of God taking away the pain, He showed me how selfish and arrogant I was to think life wasn't going to affect me. My heart was still broken, but I'm learning to live day to day.
>
> I'm enjoying life instead of controlling life and living within certain parameters. Prompted by your book and the song "Dive" by Stephen Curtis Chapman, I decided to put my life back together. I began doing small things and taking time for myself. [One of those things was taking climbing lessons and climbing the Grand Tetons!] I thought I needed to live or be a certain way, but God doesn't want that. He wants me to be me. It's amazing what a relief it is not to be in control!

Brenda changed! Change didn't necessarily feel good at the time. It didn't come naturally; it took work, courage, and commitment. But she made changes that made living her life worthwhile. It has helped her enjoy motherhood, even though that experience includes facing her worst fear. Brenda has discovered that with God as her guide, she can find joy in the toil of life.

Are you ready for the change? Changing will include letting go of many people, things, and events that you have clung to in the past. It will mean seeing your life from an eternal perspective. It will also require getting down and dirty with the reality of your life. You will start by taking inventory of your time, then move to looking at your money and spending, your energy, your spiritual life, and more. So let's get practical about living a life that matters.

START BY TAKING INVENTORY

Taking inventory of your life is one of the most important tasks required for discovering what is important. Take a deep, long look at what you do when you aren't paying attention. Now, don't get all spiritual on me and try to add extra devotions and mission trips into your day the week you take inventory. Just track your ordinary, getting up, going to work, doing laundry, watching television, going about your business, everyday life, and see how you spend your time.

How to Take Inventory of Your Life

For the next week, write down the number of hours you spend in different areas of your life. Make your record at a time that works best for you—morning, night, whenever. If you don't write down what you are doing at least daily, you will lose track of what you actually did and how much time it took. (That's a lesson in itself about how fleeting our days really are.)

Every day is important. You would think you could remember what you did with the 24 hours you had two days ago, but when I did this exercise, I found I could not. I couldn't remember how long I had slept.

I could recall the big events and regular occurrences, but there were a lot of hours I couldn't account for. Isn't it amazing that you could live for years, and wake up one morning and not really know how you had lived? Don't let that happen to you. Take an honest, brave look at your life. This exercise is just between you and God and anyone else with whom you wish to share it. Be honest, be accountable, be amazed.

	Sun.	Mon.	Tues.	Wed.	Thurs.	Fri.	Sat.	**TOTAL**
Sleeping:								
Working:								
Grooming:								
In the car:								
Errands:								
Household chores:								
Watching TV:								
Reading:								
Spending time with God:								
Resting:								
Exercising:								
Eating:								
Church:								
Entertainment:								
Talking on phone:								
Other:								

Matching Your Time with Your Priorities

It's always surprising to recognize how you spend much of your time. Hebrews 2:1 says that we need to pay careful attention to what we have heard, or we will drift away. Paying careful attention to your life will help you discover how the life you are living may not match the priorities you value.

When I did this exercise and led some other women through this process, most of us were surprised by the way we spent our time. Nearly all of us could find better ways to use our lives. For example, I realized I spent a lot of time watching TV and driving in the car. But what surprised us most was that many things we did, activities we took for granted, were actually things Jesus is looking for in a life well lived. We were all afraid to take this inventory at first, but some of us experienced confirmation and appreciation of what God is doing in our lives.

Time Passes

The purpose of this exercise isn't to create a time schedule so you can feel guilt-free about what you do; rather it should help you see the value of a day—or even two minutes.

My British friends would cringe at the way I make tea. I take my tea bag, plop it into a coffee mug, add water, and pop it into the microwave for two minutes. This is a regular practice for me, and over the years I have been amazed at what I can do in the two minutes before the microwave beeps. Sometimes I can unload an entire dishwasher. Often I can make two sandwiches and get them into the lunch bag, all before time's up. Many times I just stand there staring blankly into nothingness, only to be drawn back when I hear the distant, periodic beep of the microwave letting me know that I have forgotten its contents. My lesson from the microwave is that time gives us opportunities. These opportunities may seem inconsequential, but they can add up to a lot. I'm not trying to motivate super-Christians here and I'm certainly not telling you that you should fill every minute, but I do want to encourage you to pay more attention to God's gift of time.

Does your life reflect God's priorities? If I were to come to your home and look around, would I immediately be able to perceive the priorities God has given you? Would I recognize your priorities as I looked over your calendar?

Having the right priorities doesn't mean that everyone will be happy with you. That was certainly Jesus' experience. He came to this earth to pursue His passion, yet over and over people were disappointed by His focus. Judas wanted Him to bring about an earthly kingdom. The religious leaders were indignant that He claimed to be God's Son. Peter thought He should never talk about dying. But Jesus didn't allow other people to draw Him away from what He knew God was calling Him to do.

As you look at your life and compare it to the way God wants you to live, don't be afraid to make changes. My husband's grandmother used to say, "If you aim for the stars, you might just reach the roof, but if you aim at the roof, you might not make it off the ground." God made you in such a way that your priorities for serving Him are different from mine, but they are no less important. When you know those priorities and follow God's leading, you will be amazed at what He can do through you.

God gives you the passion to serve Him, and He provides everything you need so that your service will honor Him. God has provided the wisdom for all the books and articles I've written, the messages I've shared, and the people I have counseled. My husband's grandma also said, "If you are going to dream, you might as well dream big. It won't cost you any more." Let God dream big in you. Set out to glorify Him, and heaven only knows how you will end up. One thing I know for sure, you will be happy with and proud of your life.

God Is Gracious

God is completely gracious and kind to us in the matters we've been considering. God isn't like some Olympic judges who must count the exact tenth of a second to determine worthiness. I'm always amazed how one Olympic athlete can finish a race one tenth of a second behind the athlete in front and walk away without a prize. God doesn't do that. I meet so many people caught up in whether or not they spend one hour a day with God. Often they avoid spending time with God altogether because they don't think they have an hour to give to God daily. I tell people to spend 10 minutes of quality time with God, and it will transform their lives. Some days I only have 10 minutes, but God can do a powerful work in my life in those few minutes. He knows my heart, and when I have an open heart, the amount of time is not the issue.

The time inventory shouldn't become a legalistic exercise; I'm not trying to turn you into a clone of me or somebody else. Its goal is to help you clearly see the gift of your life and effectively use it to glorify God and please Jesus.

Getting the Right Things Right

Carolyn took a time inventory and realized that an area of her life she was afraid would be a time problem was actually an area that glorified God. Carolyn loves to talk. She talks on the phone, visits with her neighbors, and chats with the woman behind her in the grocery store checkout line. She gets a lot of ribbing from her husband and others who know about her love for communication. Carolyn hated to be honest on her inventory, worried about the wave of shame and guilt that might swamp her after acknowledging the hours she talked each day.

Adding them up, she was embarrassed to see she spent five hours on the phone each week and seven hours visiting with friends. That was a lot of time—12 hours of talking a week. But the Holy Spirit helped her see that her visits were a blessing. She encouraged her mother over the phone, and her friends gained human connection and the assurance that they were loved. Activities some people had made her feel ashamed about were validated by God Himself.

For the first time, Carolyn actually felt no guilt for enjoying phone conversations and visits with friends. She saw through God's eyes how these actions were ministries. While she wasn't the kind of missionary who raised support and went to a distant country, she was a missionary in her own hometown, with her own telephone.

A Time to Clean the Toilet

What is the last thing many women want to do, but they do anyway? How about cleaning a toilet? It takes time to clean a toilet well. How can that task be important or amount to anything good?

Wise King Solomon laments the realities of time when he writes in Ecclesiastes 3:1-8:

> There is a time for everything,
> and a season for every activity under heaven:
> a time to be born and a time to die,
> a time to plant and a time to uproot,
> a time to kill and a time to heal,
> a time to tear down and a time to build,
> a time to weep and a time to laugh,
> a time to mourn and a time to dance,
> a time to scatter stones and a time to gather them,
> a time to embrace and a time to refrain,
> a time to search and a time to give up,
> a time to keep and a time to throw away,
> a time to tear and a time to mend,
> a time to be silent and a time to speak,
> a time to love and a time to hate,
> a time for war and a time for peace.

As we evaluate our lives and the time we are spending, let's consider the wisdom of Solomon on this very subject. What would King Solomon advise women as they evaluate their inventory? What would he advise about the cleaning of the toilet? Would he suggest hiring a maid? Leaving it dirty? Cleaning it yourself?

Many years ago as I was spending time with God while cleaning my house, He gave me this very true and humbling insight: As I knelt down beside the toilet bowl to scrub it, God showed me that I deserved much worse than this humbling position. If I really thought about it, as humble and lowly as I felt kneeling down by a toilet, my posture didn't compare with what my sin merited. There was a devotional thought born beside the toilet bowl.

Living a life that counts isn't about doing a specific list of things. It isn't about being the richest, most famous, most important person on this earth. It is about living life well, whether anyone else notices or not. It is about recognizing that the things of God are the things that will last forever. Those are the things in which I want to invest my life. I don't want to be found pursuing a million dollars when Jesus Christ returns for me. I would rather be giving a cup of cool water in His name, because I know that is the kind of pursuit that will last forever.

God wants to bring to your life the beauty mentioned in Ecclesiastes 3. He makes all things beautiful in His time (v. 11). That's the kind of life I want. Remember, there's a time for everything under heaven.

A Time for Beauty

In every woman's life, there is:

a time to scrub a toilet and a time to attend a gala,

a time to get her hair done and a time to wash the hair of a dirty beggar,

a time to quietly connect to God and a time to boldly proclaim her love for Him,

a time to store away money for retirement and a time to give extravagantly to a missionary,

a time to have lunch with a friend and a time to be alone with God and study His Word diligently,

a time to watch TV and a time to eagerly watch for His coming.

He and He alone is the key to making all things beautiful in their time.

It's time to make some changes in your life. Let's journey together into new ideas about how to spend the time you have while you live on earth. Let's listen to how God longs for you to live your life.

Journal Exercise

1. Keep a journal of how you spend your time. Follow the instructions on pages 43-44.
2. After you have taken a week of inventory, it will be time to evaluate your life. Are you getting enough rest and sleep? We will talk about this later because it is essential to making meaningful changes. Are you surprised by how much time you watch TV? Now, it's time to evaluate your results in light of God's perspective of time. Follow these steps as you read through your inventory.

   Step 1. Highlight the time you spend that is inflexible. For example, you work 40 hours a week, you have certain chores that have to be done, you need your sleep, etc.

   Step 2. Put a star by anything you spend your time on that God rewards. From the preprinted list it would include: any chores, work, or so on that you do for the glory of God, spiritual disciplines, time you spend in relationships to honor God, defending or standing up for the faith, spending money for eternal purposes, spending time studying and treasuring God's Word, time spent watching for Jesus' coming.

   Step 3. Circle activities that you feel waste your time. Don't be too strict with yourself. For instance, I think some of my TV watching is helpful to me, yet I've seen where I could easily cut that time in half and put those hours to better use. I might even use it to rest in a way that is more edifying to me, such as reading or walking my dog.

3. Now that you have recorded your daily activities, examine where you spend your time and think about the changes you would like to make.
   - What time expenditures do you not want to change?
   - What would you like to be doing with your time that you're not currently doing?
   - What areas of your life need more time? (Examples: sleep, exercise, reading, relaxing.)

- What areas of your life consume too much time? (Examples: shopping, talking on the phone, watching television.)
- In what ways are you using your time to please Jesus?

Goal for the Week

Think of the time you dread most this week (doing laundry, cleaning house, working, etc.) and write a proverb contrasting it with something you enjoy. Memorize it and remember it when you are doing the thing you dread.

There is a time to (thing you dread) and a time to (thing you enjoy).

Part Two

Get Set!
How Do I Live
a Life that Counts?

Chapter Five

A New Strategy for Change

*So that you may be able to discern what is best and
may be pure and blameless until the day of Christ,
filled with the fruit of righteousness that comes through
Jesus Christ—to the glory and praise of God.*
PHILIPPIANS 1:10-11

ow do people change? My vocation of Christian counseling is
devoted to that question. Over the years I have counseled
many people who were highly motivated to make changes in their lives.
Some came because they were struggling with depression, others fought
an eating disorder, and some sought marriage therapy. Almost every person who came to me wanted to have a different life. They wanted to
change.

Not everyone I met with, however, made the changes they sought.
Some left without ever changing because they didn't want to do the hard
work that it required. If only I had magic dust that I could sprinkle over
individuals when they come into my office, I would be the most effective counselor around. Unfortunately, though, change is not that easy.

Personally, I am bewildered by change. Sometimes I will be sitting
across from a couple filled with so much hate, hostility, and conflict I
am sure they will end up divorced. Rather than tell them my gut

instinct, I apply specific tools and principles to help them resolve their conflict. Surprisingly, several months later, change has taken place. Other couples seem to have the basis of a good relationship, yet they don't make the changes needed to keep their marriage honoring to God.

I know that God uses me as an instrument of change in people's lives. Sometimes He has the individual I am counseling hear something I never said—or at least don't remember saying. A woman might tell me how a particular statement I made in the last session changed her life. When she repeats what I said, I never remember saying it.

Change is mysterious. God is mysterious and He is behind any real, lasting, and genuine change we make in our lives.

Let me illustrate this by first admitting that how a garbage disposal gets fixed is a mystery to me. In our home, when it wouldn't work, someone would get the broom, stick the end in the disposal, turn it a bit, take it out, then start the disposal again. After I grew up and had my own home, any time the garbage disposal would get stuck, I would call on my handy husband to fix it. He did the same thing as the others. One day I was home early in the morning when the garbage disposal quit working. I didn't want to wait for Brian, so I got the broom, stuck the end in the disposal, turned it around, took it out, then turned on the disposal. It worked! I didn't know how. It was a mystery to me.

Change is like that. You can follow basic steps and do what God's Word tells you to do, but experiencing real, genuine change is a miracle.

God, I'm Powerless

The most powerful prayer I have ever prayed is, "God, I am powerless." This full and complete admission of my utter inability to alter my life becomes the catalyst for the mysterious actions of change. This is a book about changing your life. Yet the kind of change that really counts is not directly under your control. Yes, there is a lot of work that you need to do to move toward this change, but there's also a lot you can't do either—if you want real, genuine, Holy Spirit–filled change. If this is the kind of change you are seeking, I've got good news and bad news. The bad news is that you cannot accomplish it on your own. The good news is that God promises to do it in you.

Agents of Change

Change agent #1: Imitation. Paul was constantly inviting believers to imitate the way he lived his life (Philippians 4:9). Probably no one heeded this invitation more than Timothy. Timothy was like a son to Paul (1 Timothy 1:2, 18; 2 Timothy 1:2; 2:1). Paul could trust him completely with the leadership responsibilities in the church. He was a faithful companion and Paul mentored him and led by example.

People often follow our example, whether we want them to or not. I used to drive in Dallas traffic 30 minutes each way to take my children to school. God used this time to teach me the powerful lesson of imitation.

One day while we were driving, a car pulled over too closely and my daughter said, "Watch it, you jerk!" I looked at her and wondered, *Where did she learn that?* It would be easy to blame that one on my husband, but I had to face the facts. I was the one she was imitating. She was only 10 years old. What kind of example was I setting? I've really been trying to change this area of my life, and I confess that I wish I were more relaxed about things. But I am teaching my children that I am wrong to react that way. They, in turn, keep me accountable, which I have asked them to do. They will be driving soon, and I don't want them getting upset by rude drivers. I need to be the kind of example they can imitate. As my poor example illustrates, imitation in itself isn't enough for real change.

Change agent #2: Accountability. Accountability provides a powerful impetus for change. When I know that next week I will have to face my accountability group about my goals, I try a little harder to reach them. Moses' relationship with his father-in-law demonstrated the power of accountability (Exodus 18:17-23). We don't know much about Moses' father-in-law except that he wasn't Jewish. Moses was having a huge problem leading the nation. There were endless lines of individuals with complaints they needed Moses to resolve. Moses was not God; he was merely a man, and trying to solve every little dispute in the country was literally impossible.

God used Moses' father-in-law, Jethro, to help. Jethro told Moses to make an organizational chart of leaders in the nation and establish chains of leadership and responsibilities for the people to follow when they had a complaint.

Moses' accountability to his father-in-law yielded good results. But, accountability alone would never have enabled him to lead the nation of Israel as effectively as he did. Moses was not only accountable to Jethro, he was also accountable to God. For real, genuine change to take place, we need to have ultimate accountability to God.

Change agent #3: Hitting bottom. Some of us feel that we have hit bottom too often in our lives. It's amazing how far down some people have to get before genuine change results. Jonah is an example of hitting bottom for sure (Jonah 1–4).

God had invited Jonah to change, and Jonah wanted none of it. He was pretty satisfied with his prejudices against the horrid bottom dwellers in Nineveh, and he was not willing to follow God's orders to invite them to repentance. He got on a ship and headed for Tarshish (modern day Spain). There was a violent storm that stirred up a group of hardened sailors who then cried out to their gods. Jonah knew that the storm was a message from the One True God, so he told them to drop him out of the ship and the storm would cease. At first the sailors didn't want to, but as the waves kept raging, they finally complied. Jonah would rather have drowned in that ocean than obey God. Now that's resistance to change!

God's plan wasn't for Jonah to die, but to give him a second chance, so He had Jonah swallowed by a large fish. Can you imagine hitting bottom any further than finding yourself alive inside the stomach of a stinky fish? Jonah finally accepted his opportunity to change and yielded himself to God.

God's plan for Jonah hadn't changed. God still wanted him to preach in Nineveh, so He conveniently had the fish spit Jonah out on a Ninevite beach. Jonah was faithful to his word, and he did preach God's message to the Ninevites, but he wasn't happy about it.

Though Jonah's story illustrates how hitting bottom can be a catalyst for change, it also shows us that hitting bottom won't necessarily bring about genuine change. After Jonah preached to the Ninevites and got the whole country to repent, he reverted to his old prejudiced, angry-at-God self.

Change agent #4: Catastrophic circumstances. Catastrophic circumstances are not necessarily related to your personal behavior. For instance, September 11, 2001, created catastrophic circumstances that brought about change in thousands of people's lives. Thousands were catapulted into a personal relationship with Jesus Christ and thus changed where they will be spending eternity. We have seen a silver lining in this terrible catastrophe: Americans humbled themselves and prayed. A president led a nation to its knees. I observed a spirit of humility and repentance spread across our country.

The apostle Paul (known as Saul before his conversion) made a 180-degree turn after a catastrophic circumstance. In Acts 9 we read that Saul was minding his own business, living his life as a zealous Pharisee. He led a group of righteous Jews on a quest to wipe out those who called themselves Christians. Saul was such an effective defender of God that his name and reputation were synonymous with fear for the new followers of Christ.

Why would God want someone like Saul? Most followers of Christ saw him as the opposite of God, filled with hatred. But, God did want him, and He used a catastrophic circumstance—blindness—to bring about change in Saul's life. After using a bright light to blind Saul, Jesus asked, "Why do you persecute me?" (Acts 9:4). The whole experience literally stopped Saul in his tracks. It took blindness to open his eyes to the true spiritual realities that were happening in this world. He went from being a persecutor of Christians (as Saul) to serving as one of their most effective leaders (as Paul).

Many Christians promise to change when they are faced with trauma. They try to bargain with God, hoping He will get them out of pain and suffering. Experiencing a catastrophe and crying out to God at that moment, but not living for Him after the catastrophe is resolved, is not evidence of genuine change.

Change agent #5: Passivity. I've written about passive Christianity before. It has truly been the key to real change in my life. Some people don't like the label passive Christianity, because the word *passive* conjures up negative thoughts. I'm going to use it anyway, because people also don't like to practice passive Christianity. It goes against our whole sense of being human. We think we have to do, to perform, to be what God wants us to be. I've tried that. I've memorized verses; I've prayed the Jabez prayer; I've read my Bible and gone to Bible studies. I've been a very active Christian and still haven't received the change my heart so desires.

Henry Drummond states, "We are changed; we do not change ourselves. No man can change himself. Throughout the New Testament wherever these moral and spiritual transformations are described the verbs are in the passive voice. Passive means not active, but acted upon, affected by an outside force."[1]

Henry Drummond provides wonderful illustrations of how true, genuine change happens in our lives. Just like a thermometer changes because something outside of the thermometer creates this change, so it is in the soul of man. There are invisible pressures outside of the soul of man that create genuine change. He writes, "We are subject to a transforming influence. We do not transform ourselves."[2]

If you haven't figured it out yet, let me explain. This world is full of mystery. Actually, the whole Christian life is a bit mysterious. The mystery of the garbage disposal, which I mentioned earlier, can be explained by a plumber. But some mysteries can never be explained. Though God reveals Himself and His plan in His Word, there's much He keeps to Himself. I can only trust that it is for my good that I don't get to know every detail. The best spiritual decision I ever made was to enter into this mystery with all the passivity I could muster.

I'm writing a book about how to change your life, but I'm telling you that if you desire true, genuine change, you need to be passive. Now what's up with that? I'll try to explain. I'm inviting you into a life of passivity. If you really want to live a life that matters, you can't succeed without fully relying on God.

Drummond encourages Christians to see themselves as mirrors that reflect God's glory. "A mirror does not create images, it only reflects. We are like a mirror. As we focus on Christ, the reflection of His character transforms us into His image. It is a process—from character to character—from a poor character to a better one, from a better one to a little better still, from that to one still more complete, until by slow degrees the perfect image is attained. The solution of the problem of sanctification is compressed into a sentence: Reflect the character of Christ and you will become like Christ."[3]

I don't want to motivate a whole army of "doing" women through this book. I suspect you may have chosen this book so you can find how you can "do" better in your life. Perhaps you hoped it would offer ideas for "doing" more successfully. And indeed it does offer the most proven ingredient for living a meaningful life: The answer is to build an intimate relationship with God so that He is doing the "doing."

I hope I don't have you totally confused, but the new strategy for change is to rest. Jesus Himself said it: "Come to me, all you who are weary and burdened, and I will give you rest. Take my yoke upon you and learn from me, for I am gentle and humble in heart, and you will find rest for your souls. For my yoke is easy and my burden is light" (Matthew 11:28-30).

I meet so many women who are burdened because of the yokes they are wearing—their husband's yoke, their mother's yoke, their children's. They think they are wearing God's yoke too, yet their heavy burdens show they are not wearing God's yoke. Jesus said that His yoke is light.

If you are trying to balance your life in the right way, it shouldn't feel burdensome. Just a few minutes ago I was doing my task for my Sunday school class, writing notes to visitors. As I started to write the notes, I thought, *I really should be teaching a class rather than doing this, because I have gifts for teaching God's Word.*

Rather than rush to sign up to teach, I asked God, "Would You rather have me teaching?"

Immediately I heard in my heart, "This is the job I have for you."

Teaching every Sunday, while I do all the other things God has called me to do in my church, would be a burden for me. The ministries that I am involved in at my church and in my community require sacrifice, time, and effort. However, they are not burdens, because when I am doing what God has called me to do, He actually does this work through me. If I try to take on something else just because I know I can do it, my yoke begins to choke me.

How to Change

My pastor told this parable:

> A mountain climber, proud and self-reliant, set out on a hard climb. As night fell, he refused to make camp but continued his trek. There was no moon and the stars were covered by the clouds.
>
> As he was climbing a ridge about 100 meters from the top, he slipped and fell. Careening rapidly, he could see only blotches of darkness as he felt the terrible sensation of gravity sucking him to the earth. He was certain he would die.
>
> But then he felt a jolt that almost tore him in half. Like any good mountain climber, he had staked himself with a long rope tied to his waist. In those moments of stillness, in the blackness of the dark night, suspended in the air, this self-reliant, self-made man had no choice to but shout into the air, "God, please help me!"
>
> Suddenly he heard a deep voice from heaven: "What do you want me to do?"
>
> "Save me!" said the climber.
>
> "Do you really think that I can save you?" God asked.
>
> "Yes!" the climber replied.
>
> "Then cut the rope that is holding you up," God directed.
>
> There was silence and stillness. The man held tighter and tighter still to his rope. The next day the rescue team found a frozen mountain climber holding strongly to a rope, three feet off the ground.[4]

The simple formula for effective change is balancing your effort with God's ability. The best explanation I can share is Philippians 2:12-13: "Therefore, my dear friends, as you have always obeyed—not only in my presence, but now much more in my absence—continue to work out your salvation with fear and trembling, for it is God who works in you to will and to act according to his good purpose."

We are told to work out our own salvation with fear and trembling in verse 12. That seems like a works salvation, but you must not miss verse 13, which explains that it is *God* who works in you both to will and to do His good pleasure. You could not even will to live your life better if it weren't for God working in you.

This is humbling and at the same time freeing. What this means is that the more you rely on God, the closer you will get to genuine change. It's the greatest mystery of the Christian life. God tells you how to live and then helps you live that way.

What a wonderful God we serve. It's not that there's no effort in it; it's that the effort you make will never be enough and was never designed to be enough. It was Jesus' fervent prayer for us in John 17:21 that we may be one with Him as He and God are one. God longs for it, we need it, so let's stop striving. Let's stop condemning ourselves and feeling guilty about our lives. Let's give our lives fully to God and desire to live the kind of life that He wants us to live. Let's make over our lives in His power and strength.

Keep this in mind as you make decisions, take action, and continue your journey through the rest of this book. Take delight in your own powerlessness and the reality of God's strength.

Journal Exercise

1. You described your perfect life in chapter one. You've examined how God wants you to be living in chapters two and three. You looked at how you are living in chapter four. What would you do that you are not doing now, what would you not do, and how would you see your life if it had everything you wanted and everything God wanted?

2. Write a letter to God asking Him to show you His yoke for you and how to wear it with Him.

Goal for the Week

As you are working this week, imagine yourself yoked with Christ and not bearing your burden alone.

Chapter Six

Creating New Priorities

With this in mind, we constantly pray for you,
that our God may count you worthy of his calling,
and that by his power he may fulfill every good purpose
of yours and every act prompted by your faith.
2 Thessalonians 1:11

❖

*D*o you feel you need to change and desire change, but aren't sure where the change will come from? Where will you get the energy, the time, the self-control?

If you'd known Dana a year ago, today you wouldn't believe she is the same person. She looks the same, hasn't changed her hairstyle, wears the same clothes, hasn't lost weight, but she is hardly the same person. Last year she was a hard-driving executive with a large company, making lots of money. This year she is a stay-at-home mother of three teenagers—and always broke. Last year she was always anxious, feeling the pressure of the world on her shoulders. This year, she feels anxious about finding the money for her son's youth-group skiing trip, but she quickly turns her anxiety to prayer.

You can see Dana's change in the way she carries herself these days. It's the spring in her step. Last year she was on the verge of divorcing her lazy husband, who didn't make enough money to support the family. This year their marriage is better than ever, and his business has picked up.

What happened to Dana? She made meaningful changes in her life—she's had a life makeover. Through the years Dana has participated in several makeovers. Ten years ago she had a weekend of beauty at a spa and got a physical makeover, trying to relieve stress resulting from three kids, a husband, and her high-pressure job. It was nice for a weekend. However, the new hairstyle was too much to keep up with, so she went back to her old one after a month.

Dana also participated in a financial makeover about five years ago. She attended a personal finance seminar and learned about investing, quickly using her new knowledge to set up college accounts for each of her children and develop a plan to pay off the house. It helped her family become more financially independent, but it also put more job pressure on Dana, because her family needed her paycheck. The financial makeover made Dana feel a little better and a little worse at the same time.

Now Dana's life makeover has been the first makeover to give her dramatic results with eternal significance. It helped her realize how much she hated her work and the pressure it created in her life. She hated missing out on significant moments in her children's lives because she had to travel frequently. She hated hating her husband for not having a better paying job so she wouldn't feel trapped by hers. She hated feeling stuck in a life that was so unsatisfying.

Dana finally ended up in a counselor's office with major depression. As the counselor explored different areas of her life, he helped her understand the source of her depression. A prescribed antidepressant got her functioning again, but there was still a lot of work for Dana to do. She took a good, long look at her life and found ways to make changes she never considered possible. Today she is living in the freedom of those decisions and finds her toil in life much more satisfying.

Dana discovered that her depression was caused by living a life that did not fit her priorities. She didn't like anything about her job. She hated making money and couldn't enjoy the things her money bought. Asked what brought her the most pleasure in life, her answer was "spending time with family," something she never had time to do. She traveled 70 percent of each week. When she was home, she tried to go to everything she could with her children. The time with her husband was mainly spent fighting about why he couldn't get a better job. She didn't believe his claim that he couldn't fully focus on his business because the kids needed him.

Only because depression threatened to take the very life from her did Dana look at how off target her life was. She had female coworkers who liked their jobs. They were not angry that they didn't have more time with their kids. They found joy in making the kind of money and the high-risk business decisions that were a part of the position. But, Dana wasn't like them. After a marriage counseling session in which the counselor helped Dana understand that her husband could focus more on his job if she would let up, the couple decided that Dana should quit her job and stay home.

Six months after making this decision, Dana quit. She and her husband informed the kids that things were going to change financially. They sold their large house and found one they could pay off with the profit from their first home. This took some pressure off Dana's husband as the sole breadwinner. Dana was always great at finding ways to save money, and this new endeavor was a challenge that brought pleasure to her. She didn't want the kids to resent her quitting work, so she found creative ways to keep them in the sports and activities they had participated in before.

A year after leaving her job, Dana is full of joy. Life isn't easy. There are disappointments. She struggles to teach her teenagers to respect her and each other. She gets worn out carting her kids all over the place and teaching her eldest to drive. The laundry undoes her at times. But she wouldn't trade her life for the one she once lived. She finds joy in her toil because the toil brings satisfaction.

Not only is Dana happy, but her husband is making more money than ever. He didn't have to work as hard in the past because Dana always made so much money. He was subconsciously balancing her workaholism for the sake of the kids. The kids say they love their mom being home one day, and the next they say they hate it. But what else would you expect from teenagers? The great reality is that Dana is no longer depressed, and she is finally able to make her life fit her priorities.

It is tough to find satisfaction if your life doesn't fit your priorities. Too many of us live life without really thinking about what we are doing and why we are doing it.

DISCOVERING YOUR UNIQUE PRIORITIES

Deep inside each of us, God has planted His plans and desires for our lives—seeds that, if nurtured and developed in His Sonlight, will produce a meaningful life. We were created to make an impact on our world. Look around at the beauty of this world, and you will recognize that we were created by a very creative God. Because we are made in His image, part of that image is a desire to be creative like Him. Each of us expresses that creativity in a different way. We all have our own style and unique priorities.

Prompted by world events a number of years ago, I asked myself, "If I knew without a doubt that Christ would return in the year 2000, what would I want to be doing with my life?" My answer included this list:

- Stop worrying and complaining about clothes and house
- Get my bills paid
- Be more open about the way I go about my life
- Teach Bible studies
- Continue to counsel and encourage people
- Keep kids at Christian school
- Grow in character
- Continue to write books
- Grow in relationships with family and friends

These goals became my priorities. My list helped me know what to say no to and what to say yes to. I have a strong sense that God is pleased with my priorities, and I know He gives me the wisdom, strength, and ability to accomplish whatever I do for Him.

Focusing on these priorities brings peace and satisfaction to my toil on earth. It isn't always easy and I can't say I enjoy every minute that I am fulfilling them. But they give me a sense of purpose and help me avoid guilt when saying no to worthy requests that are not what God has called me to do.

What About You?

Take time to answer the first 12 questions in this chapter's journal exercise. Your answers will help reveal your priorities in life. Next, consider whether your priorities are reflected in your time inventory from chapter four.

Jesus' choices and actions reflected His priorities too. In Luke 4:18-19 Jesus gives His purpose statement: His priority is to preach good news to the poor, to proclaim freedom for prisoners and recovery of sight for the blind, and to release the oppressed. Everything Jesus did in His life reflected that priority, including suffering on the cross to make our true liberation a reality.

The further your life experiences are from your priorities, the more dissatisfied you will be with your life. The most important step you can take toward living a life that matters is to recognize your true priorities and work toward focusing your time on them.

Why don't we just naturally live according to our priorities? We all want to live life well; that's not the problem. But things get in the way. These are seven common pitfalls that keep us from living by our priorities:

1. Perfectionism and self-criticism get in the way. These two are true enemies of the soul. Even if you don't consider yourself a perfectionist in the pure sense of the word, you may be a perfectionist when it comes to setting priorities. For example, if your priority is to write, you may think, "I'll never have time to write a novel," so you never write anything.

Karla felt God leading her to write. She set up a desk with a laptop computer in her bedroom. She carved out time to write in the afternoons. But when she opened her file, no words would flow. She couldn't think of a single subject to write about.

As she tried to write, Karla couldn't stop thinking about an older woman at choir who had shared a prayer request for her daughter. Since Karla was already at her desk, she slipped out some stationery and wrote her church friend an encouraging note. It felt so good, she wrote another note to a different person.

That began a pattern of encouragement that went on for years, and eventually Karla understood that God was using her in a powerful way. She still used her computer to write committee notes and send e-mail, but her writing career never materialized. God showed her what a powerful writer she really was through her ministry of encouraging notes.

God doesn't give you the ministry you desire immediately. Sometimes He helps you define what your longing for ministry is really about. He prepares you. He watches to find you faithful in the little things before you enter a more public ministry. Are you willing to write a letter? Are you faithful to write a note? Will you put your all into a short story? Let God lead you; don't let perfectionism trap you.

Overcoming perfectionism doesn't happen after reading two simple paragraphs. It does help to identify it in your life and confront yourself with the truth.

1. Recognize how much perfectionism causes you to miss out on in life.
2. Accept that no one is perfect.
3. Tell yourself that whoever expects you to be perfect (yourself, parents, coach) is wrong.
4. Think of the person you respect most in the world (besides Jesus). Name at least one imperfection that person has.
5. Finish a project today without making it perfect.

Self-criticism is part of each of us. At the bottom of self-criticism is arrogance that makes us self-rejecting. We think we are better than we are, so we condemn ourselves. My favorite chapter in the Bible is Romans 8 and it begins: "Therefore, there is now no condemnation for those who are in Christ Jesus." Even though I feel comfortable with self-condemnation, I don't want it. I want to be free of self-condemnation. I am only free when I see myself in Christ Jesus.

Moses is famous for his self-critical statement when God called him at the burning bush (Exodus 3:11). He said, "Who am I?" God told Moses the strength to do His will would come from God Himself.

Self-condemnation comes naturally to us, while freedom from condemnation is supernatural. You are invited to lay aside self-hatred and receive the truth that you are deeply loved. "Self-rejection is the greatest enemy of the spiritual life because it contradicts the sacred voice that calls us the 'Beloved.' Being the Beloved expresses the core truth of our existence."[1]

2. Laziness gets in the way. In my counseling office I meet people who come in week after week, paying a lot of money but never carrying out the suggestions I give them. For the 45 minutes they are in my office they have high hopes of change, but after they leave, nothing happens.

They aren't morally corrupt. They aren't mentally handicapped. They are basically lazy. They don't want to put the effort required into making changes. The sad thing is that if they would start doing the hard work, the benefits of a changed life would energize them to keep going. When you are living your life in a healthy way, it begins to feel right and overcomes your laziness.

I challenged Rebecca to stay focused on her eating plan for one week. She wasn't committing to the rest of her life, just to one week. By the end of that week, she was ready to commit to another. It took starting to help her to keep going.

3. A life out of balance gets in the way. Some choose to live an insane, out-of-balance life, rather than risk saying no to anyone. If you have children, for instance, there is the activity dilemma to deal with. My son plays sports. At first we limited him to one sport a season and one music lesson, but we let him play two sports because we didn't realize that roller hockey and soccer would overlap. Then he liked them both and didn't want to quit either, so he kept on playing. We rationalized it because he wasn't taking a music lesson, but it still complicated our lives.

We know kids who play three or four sports. One of my son's friends told his mom, "When I'm a dad, it will only be one sport."

She said, "Great, let's do that with you. Which one do you want to give up?"

He didn't think it would come to that. It is so easy to get out of balance and do too much for your kids, for your church, for your friends, even for yourself.

For some of you the absolute best thing you could do is to drop everything. Some of you might be so out of balance, there is no way you could hear God reveal His plan unless you made a dramatic change like that.

4. Not working from strengths gets in the way. Balaam is a biblical character whose story perplexes me. He was a prophet of God, but why God would allow such a foolish servant to speak His truths astonishes me. Then again, He allows me to be used by Him and that astounds me also.

Balaam did not work from his strength. When asked to curse the nation of Israel by the king of Moab, he whined, "I can't; God won't let me."(See Numbers 22:13.) Though he wanted to, he knew it would be impossible to actually curse the nation of Israel, but he wasted his time trying to work a deal with the king. It took a stubborn donkey to help Balaam see how weak his plan really was (Numbers 22:28).

Balaam didn't work from his strength. He tried to use God's gift to hurt God's work (2 Peter 2:15-16). God has given every believer spiritual gifts not to make money, become famous, or look good, but in order to build up the church (1 Corinthians 12:7).

Every Christian has at least one spiritual gift, and it's important for you to know yours. (See 1 Corinthians 12:7, 11; Ephesians 4:7.) If you try to mimic another person's spiritual life, you may not be working from your strengths because your spiritual gifts may be different. (See Romans 12:3-6.) God distributes our spiritual gifts (1 Corinthians 12:11; Ephesians 4:7-8); we don't choose them ourselves. I encourage you to do a study on spiritual gifts and learn to recognize yours.

Do you realize how unique and special you are? No one else has your fingerprint. No one else has your life to live. So don't try to pattern your life after someone else's. While it is good and helpful to have mentors and guides along the journey, stay tuned to how God calls you specifically.

I have my share of weaknesses; for example, I lack the gift of hospitality. I've stressed myself out trying to put together a luncheon with special touches to make my guests feel at home and pampered. But I have many friends who can do just that with ease. It doesn't stress them the way it does me. Though hospitality is hard work, it is something for which they are uniquely gifted.

Those same friends might feel overwhelmed by having to share a devotional thought at a luncheon. Giving a devotional is easy for me because God has uniquely gifted me in this area. I can't do it on my own; the Holy Spirit inspires me to share from God's Word.

Now I'm not saying God would never ask me to provide a special luncheon, nor am I saying that my friends with gifts of hospitality would never be called upon to share devotional thoughts. I am saying I need to work from my strengths and give God room to overcome my weaknesses. I would waste a lot of time and energy trying to give parties like my friends. I need to accept who I am and let God use me in my uniqueness.

5. Fear gets in the way. Fear drove the woman from Samaria (John 4:6-7) to the well at noon. She wanted to draw water in the heat of the day, out of sight of the town gossips. Her life and choices had given them some juicy subjects to discuss. Married five times, now living with a man who was not her husband, she was a disgrace. On the outside she may have looked as if she didn't care what they thought, but deep down, she must have, or else why would she choose to draw water at such an unpleasant hour?

Fear can become paralyzing if we give it full reign in our lives. Most of us try to avoid what we fear, hiding it deep inside just like the woman from Samaria. Yet Jesus helped her face her greatest fear. He had a way of getting to the heart of the matter with each person He met. He said, "Go and get your husband." He didn't ask this of just any woman. He asked it of that woman at that particular time, because He wanted to expose her fear. The fact that she did not have a husband was the core fear of her life. She was a castaway wife, not even worthy to be married to the man she now lived with.

The woman answered this stranger by telling a truth that concealed her fear. She said, "I have no husband."

Jesus responded to her the same way He responds to you and me; He helped her confront her fear. He said, "What you say is correct; you have had five husbands, and the man you live with is not your husband."

"How did He know that?" she must have wondered.

Jesus told her "everything about herself," assuring her she was loved and accepted by Him. His words melted her fears. At the end of the conversation, she left the desolate well and ran toward the village she had bypassed. She was Jesus' witness in Samaria, telling everyone to come and meet this incredible man whose words drove out fear.

First John 4:18 says that perfect love drives out fear. It will drive out our fear of failure. Jesus' perfect love is what we need to overcome our fears about living by our true priorities.

6. Clinging to the past gets in the way. Kathryn's mother died when she was 10 years old. Her dad did the best he could raising two daughters alone, but Kathryn always felt she was missing something essential by not having a mom.

When she became a mother, Kathryn was so driven by her own longings for a mom that it led her to make poor decisions regarding her own children's needs. She volunteered for everything at her children's school and church and spent all her money on dance lessons, music lessons, and expensive clothes, trying to make up for what she never got.

Is there anything in your past blocking your ability to pursue your priorities? Are you being driven by the need for somebody's (parent, husband, boyfriend, boss) approval?

7. Not saying no can get in the way. This may be the number one reason for not making meaningful life changes. My main goal for this book is to help set women free from the prison of trying to please everyone. To follow God's plan is sure to disappoint someone. You must learn to say no to all the *good* things in the world that distract you from the *important* things God has for you to do.

Are you ready to make God's priorities your own? Galatians 6:9 says, "Let us not become weary in doing good." It's time to get practical and learn what it takes to make pursuing a life that matters a reality!

Journal Exercise

1. What priorities would you want to pursue if you knew nothing could get in the way?
2. What priorities would you focus on if you believed Jesus Christ was returning for all Christians tomorrow?
3. Do you have a secret dream that you would love to fulfill?
4. What is most important to you?
5. In what ways are you presently satisfied with how you spend time?
6. Where can you see that you are wasting time?
7. In what areas do you feel obligated to spend time, yet aren't happy doing so?
8. In these areas that you feel unhappy about, is there a way that you are missing God in them? How can you see God as part of them?
9. What is God's will for your life?
10. Where are you disobeying God's will?
11. How are you living with different priorities from those of the world?
12. How has God made all things beautiful in your life?
13. Your answers to these questions will help reveal your priorities. What are your priorities for your life?
14. Are your priorities reflected in the time you spend on your life, as covered in chapter four?
15. Evaluate which things get in the way and prevent you from doing what you know would be pleasing to Jesus. Beside each one write one or more of the issues you struggle with in these areas:
    • Perfectionism/self-criticism
    • Laziness
    • Living out of balance
    • Not working from your strengths
    • Fear
    • Clinging to the past
    • Not saying no at the right time

16. What can you do this week to make your life conform to what Jesus would want?

Goal for the Week

Make a special note to yourself whenever you give time to one of your priorities this week. Imagine Christ smiling at you.

Part Three

Go! Living Your New Life

Chapter Seven

Finding the Energy to Live a Life that Counts

For physical training is of some value,
but godliness has value for all things,
holding promise for both the present life
and the life to come.
1 TIMOTHY 4:8

$\mathcal{M}$y wedding wasn't a disaster from the start, but somehow the week before, little things began to fall apart. First my dad had a fender bender. Then the typically balmy Florida weather went sour and several friends' flights were canceled or redirected. I was feeling a little feverish and discovered I had strep throat.

By the rehearsal dinner we had found everybody at the airports, I had started taking antibiotics, and things seemed to be getting better. The morning of the wedding, my mom's glasses broke and she had to resort to holding them together with tape, my voice was gone, and the candles wouldn't light.

Finally, two o'clock came, and I was all ready to walk down the aisle, but they held me off for another half hour. I finally found out that someone had hit a power line and the electricity was out in half of the church. (Ironically, my father was an executive at the power company. The part of the church without electricity included the outlets that powered the organ. After a 30-minute delay, the organist compromised by banging away at the piano keys. There was no way to play that organ without power.

There's also no way to energize your life without power. I remember the first time I was in charge of the way I energized my life, the summer after high school graduation. I was working part-time, involved in a part-time ministry, and had a full social calendar. The one day off from the ministry, I worked a full day, so I ended up with no days off, late nights, and little sleep. I was doing lots of good things. I wasn't doing anything that I didn't want to do. But it soon got the best of me. I came down with a severe case of mono and almost didn't get the medical release to start my first semester of college.

I learned a very important lesson. My doctor warned that there would be no all-nighters in college, and I had to promise to get eight hours of sleep every night. This helped me become a disciplined person. Out of respect for my body, I started studying for tests days ahead of time and always had papers and projects completed before the due dates. I knew I couldn't wait until the last minute.

RESPECTING YOUR BODY

God created us with the need for food, rest, and exercise to energize our lives. We won't be physically able to live a life that matters if we don't respect our energy needs.

You may be one of those women like Emma, described in the first chapter. She was going without sleep, healthful food, and exercise because she couldn't fit it in while she was being everything for her husband, children, best friend, and everybody else. Before long Emma would crash and find her reserve tank depleted. She needed to learn to respect her bodily limitations, and so do you.

You are made up of body, mind, and soul. Each of these areas has energy resources that power life. If you are neglecting any of the three you will discover that you are depleted and unmotivated to pursue a life that counts. Emma couldn't change her life until she made her energy a priority rather than an afterthought.

We all know that food, exercise, and rest are necessary ingredients for a healthy body. But because women are so centered on relationships, it is too easy to neglect these areas of their lives. It takes work, effort, and time management to attend to your physical needs. Women may feel vain or selfish if they make time to care for their bodies properly. It may require creative juggling to take care of yourself, but it will benefit your family, too. You will be in a better mood and end up being able to give more to those you love.

Food

Because women are busy, they feel justified in grabbing a quick candy bar or something just as unhealthful, rather than eating a well-balanced meal. It is hard work to deny yourself foods that are quick, easy, and tempting. Certain times of the month you may crave fatty foods and chocolate. Some women are actually addicted to food. Food can be used to replace a best friend, stuff emotions, or distract from reality. If you are going to live a meaningful life, you need to think about how to eat, exercise, and care for your body in a healthful way.

First take a look at your eating habits. You either build up energy to fuel your life, or drain your energy by the way you eat. How would you evaluate your eating? Do you take vitamins? Do you choose wisely from the food pyramid? Do you eat only when you are hungry in order to energize your life? Do you find pleasure in food? I hope you can say yes to each of those questions.

If you can't answer yes, what are you going to do about your eating habits? Why don't you do those things for your body that you know you ought to do? Is it because you don't really think of food as a source of energy? Is it because to you food is escape, pleasure, or perhaps a best friend? Do you have a wrong perspective on food?

Look around and you will see a multitude of individuals who don't view food as a delicious energy source, but rather as a means to push down negative emotions, a reward for living an unfulfilling life, a way to pass the time. It isn't the focus of this book to break through issues blocking you from using food as a tool leading to health and pleasure, the way God designed it. As you seek to live a balanced life, you may discover that an unhealthy relationship with food holds you back from experiencing all God wants for you. If that's the case, I hope these words will motivate you to attempt to move beyond your addiction to food.

You can take steps to become healthy in this area of your life. You can read a book, join a support group, or make an appointment for counseling. When you have a food addiction, you often feel you should be able to conquer it on your own. Don't block your growth in this area by assigning yourself paralyzing goals. Reach out for prayer, at a minimum, as you try to conquer your emotional eating. God doesn't condemn you for this problem. He longs to help you break out of the prison of emotional eating.

Stress

Stress is an enemy of living a meaningful life. Many of us live on an adrenaline rush. God designed our bodies to need adrenaline for specific reasons. The adrenal gland goes into action when you encounter a dangerous situation and you need a power boost to save your life. It is designed to be used occasionally, for a short period. If you live your life under constant stress, you will end up with health problems. Your body simply cannot handle continual stress; it will eventually wear out and deplete you of energy.

Signs that you are energizing your life with stress are:
- not having a regular sleep cycle;
- never getting to the end of your to-do list;
- using caffeine, sugar, and junk food to keep you going;
- eating meals in the car, at your desk, or while working;
- frequently checking in at the office and at home;
- checking voice mail or e-mail at all times of day and night.

If you are energizing your life with stress, you need to slow down. If you are living on adrenaline, you will soon discover that a crash is in your future. Eventually this type of stress will produce health issues such as chest pain, anxiety attacks, ulcers, insomnia, and other problems. The best way to avoid this crash isn't to do more, but to slow down. When you slow down, you end up able to do more in the end.

If this describes your life, make some decisions today to change your mode of operation. If you don't, eventually you will be forced to when your body can't handle it any longer.

Rest

There are cycles in women's lives when they are sleep-deprived, especially when they have young children. Then there are the teenage years when they can't totally rest until all the kids are safely home. Many women cannot spend time alone with God unless they get up an hour before everyone else in the house. Some women choose to give up needed sleep to be more "productive." This can backfire over time, because lack of sleep can deplete serotonin, a chemical our brains need for mental health.

How much sleep do you get each night? Is it enough? Are you depriving yourself of sleep? God didn't have to create us with such a legitimate need for rest, but He did. And He demonstrated rest right from the beginning. The God who never sleeps nor slumbers (Psalm 121:3-4) rested on the seventh day of creation (Genesis 2:1-4).

Rest is partly sleep, partly renewal, and partly revival for the soul. It is even good to rest from your exercise program from time to time. There is never a time that I feel the full benefits of rest more than after a week or two off from work. I love my work as a counselor; I love helping people and I don't get tired of using the gifts God has given me. I don't even realize that I'm burning out until I take an annual vacation and come back to work the first day. It amazes me how excited and ready I am to do the job that God has called me to after a bit of rest.

You may have to schedule your rest, because otherwise you might never find time for it. Try taking a quiet retreat. This type of retreat may or may not be provided by your own church. If not, look to other spiritual communities who offer simple retreats providing time to worship and commune with God.

Exercise

Next, evaluate your exercise. Are you sedentary? Do you give your body at least 30 minutes of aerobic activity three times a week? There is a big difference between being obsessed with your looks and taking care of the body God gave you. Today's lifestyle doesn't provide the exercise our bodies need from ordinary daily activity. Jesus never went to an aerobics class. He walked so much He didn't need to. Most of our lives are different.

You can do many little things in your daily life to promote good health. Park farther away from the entrance and enjoy a brisk walk to your destination, or take the stairs rather than the elevator. Cleaning your house, taking a brisk 10-minute walk, playing tag with your kids, washing your car, mowing the lawn, or gardening are fun opportunities to exercise. You can take a three-mile walk with your husband or your prayer partner. You can swim laps at the pool. Whatever motivates you and fits into your lifestyle is the best program to follow. Remember, exercising actually creates energy.

Over the years I have become more committed to my exercise program. It helped to start out slowly, exercising 15 minutes a day. Since I have a tendency to avoid exercise, I make it the first activity of my day.

I want to encourage you to energize your life through exercise by committing to a program for one month. Make sure you choose a program that fits into your life. Ask a friend to join you if you think it will help. To create a sense of accountability, tell others what you are doing. After a month check your progress and reward yourself for a job well done.

Kate was like me; she hated the thought of exercise. Her weight wasn't a problem, and she didn't want to worry about adding one more thing to her life. Her best friend, Barbara, asked if she would like to become a prayer partner and power walk through their neighborhood while praying for the community. Kate wasn't too motivated by the idea of power walking, but she did want to work on her prayer life, and she thought of Barbara as a great mentor for prayer.

Kate discovered several benefits to the power walking she did with Barbara. After about a month, she found herself sleeping better, with more energy to face her day. After a year she noticed that her thigh muscles were firmer and stronger. She was thrilled with her new ministry of intercessory prayer. God let Barbara and Kate see the fruit of their prayer in many ways. A neighbor they had prayed for received salvation. Kate doesn't think of her prayer walking as exercise for her body; she prefers to focus on the spiritual discipline and benefit. God has blessed her efforts spiritually, but He has also given her the added benefit of increased energy and better health.

General Wellness

Another area to consider when it comes to your body is whether you follow the prevention strategies recommended by your doctor. Are you getting an annual checkup? Do you have a mammogram as suggested for your age/risk for breast cancer?

Keeping your body healthy is part of your responsibility for living a life that matters. Women are more willing to go to the doctor and follow the instructions given than men are, but all too often women treat their health as an afterthought, important only when everything else is under control. Make your health a priority in order to get your life under control.

Making time for eating nutritious food, getting appropriate rest and exercise, and ridding your life of undue stress is vital to living with meaning and purpose.

Simple Tips for Energizing Your Life

1. Begin your day with stretching. Soon after you get out of bed, take a deep breath as you reach your arms to the ceiling, then breathe out slowly as you release your breath. Repeat this three to 10 times before you get into the shower. You can make it a spiritual exercise too as you praise God for one blessing with each stretch.

2. Schedule time for a 10-minute walk every day. This can be a time to exercise your dog or intercede for your neighbors if you like.

3. Don't skip breakfast. You need it for the energy to face the day. Include fiber and complex carbohydrates, such as a whole-grain cereal or toast.

4. Cut down on caffeine. If your body needs caffeine to keep going, you are probably not getting enough rest.

5. Take a multiple vitamin. Many women don't get enough nutrients due to poor diets, and stress can deplete vitamin stores. Taking your daily vitamins can help ensure good health.

6. Drink lots of water. Being dehydrated can cause fatigue.

7. Take a mini-vacation when you can. On a very stressful day, find five minutes to close your eyes, relax, and think about floating along a river or relaxing in some other peaceful place. This activity can actually lower your blood pressure and help you reenter your day with renewed focus.

8. Schedule time for play. Make sure your life is balanced with down time so you can ride a bike, fly a kite, sit by a pond, read a book, or play with a child.

9. Keep healthy. Even a cold or allergy congestion can decrease oxygen intake and increase fatigue.

10. Learn to power nap. Just 20 to 30 minutes of sleep in the early afternoon can revitalize you for the rest of the day.

11. Create a regular sleep cycle. Establish a routine to go to bed and wake up at the same time each day. Most adults require around eight hours of sleep a day.

Remember, living a life that matters is measured by the amount of time you have here on earth to live in the body. Live your life in such a way that you can get the best quality of life and longest amount of time. Always remember that God is in charge of your days and will decide how many days you will have on this earth (Psalm 139:16), but get the most out of your body to fulfill your purpose in the kingdom of God!

Journal Exercise

1. On a scale of 1 (poor) to 10 (excellent), state how well you care for your body.
2. Describe how you are taking care of your body in the following areas:
    Food
    Rest
    Stress
    Exercise
    General wellness
3. What improvements do you need to make in these areas?
    Food
    Rest
    Stress
    Exercise
    General wellness
4. Make short- and long-term goals to take better care of your body.
    This week I will . . .
    In the next six months I will . . .
    My goals to take care of my body for life are:
    Food
    Rest

Stress
Exercise
General wellness

Goal for the Week

Once a day, reach down and touch your toes, then raise your hands to the sky and praise God for your body.

Chapter Eight

Making Over
Your Mind

*Blessed are you when people insult you, persecute you
and falsely say all kinds of evil against you because of me.
Rejoice and be glad, because great is your reward
in heaven, for in the same way they persecuted
the prophets who were before you.*

Matthew 5:11-12

*D*on't underestimate the power your thoughts have over your energy each day. Some women sabotage themselves by allowing negative thoughts to constantly run through their minds. Many women can identify, never feeling like they are doing enough. There's a constant voice in their heads saying how much more they should be doing, never allowing a sense of freedom and completion.

If Lisa could tape record her mind, she would understand why she feels at the end of her rope. She is consumed with negative thoughts. Here's an example:

Your house is so plain; you need to get some color on those walls.
You probably made Josey feel unwelcome at the Bible study when
you didn't get over there soon enough to welcome her. What in the
world are you going to make for dinner? You should just go ahead

and eat that ice cream since you are so fat anyway. You need to get
the laundry done, play with your two-year-old, make a grocery list,
write out directions for the sitter, finish our will for your husband,
and balance the checkbook—and you only have two hours to do it.
Why do you waste so much time watching TV?

Just a few minutes of such thoughts and aren't you ready to turn the
tape recorder off? Who would want to hear more of that?

This is the most critical aspect of whether your efforts to change will
be successful. You have to train your mind to think differently. Your
brain is one of the most powerful and complicated organs God created,
and you will never maintain successful life changes without learning to
use your mind to connect your emotions to truth. Transforming your
mind is essential to your inner peace.

When Paul suggested a makeover to the church at Rome, he called
first for a makeover of the mind. Romans 12:1-2 says, "Therefore, I
urge you, brothers, in view of God's mercy, to offer your bodies as living sacrifices, holy and pleasing to God—this is your spiritual act of
worship. Do not conform any longer to the pattern of this world, but
be transformed by the renewing of your mind. Then you will be able
to test and approve what God's will is—his good, pleasing and perfect
will." The kind of transformation that you are seeking starts in your
mind.

Most women I know are in need of some serious mind makeovers.
Too often women live their lives based on their feelings, and one of the
most negative feelings behind women's decisions is guilt. Women think
they need to be everything to everybody, and they feel guilty when they
fail to give everyone what they want.

WHAT WAS I THINKING?

"What was I thinking?" is a question women often ask themselves too
late, when they are in the middle of their overcommitted messes.

"What was I thinking when I told my sister I could keep her kids
for a whole week during my finals at school?"

"What was I thinking when I told the pastor I would decorate the whole church in the two hours between the Scout meeting and the Founders Banquet?"

"What was I thinking when I spent a thousand dollars more than my budget to make my kids happy at Christmas?"

"What was I thinking when I promised my son I would buy him that computer game when I don't even have enough money to pay the electric bill?"

"What was I thinking when I let my daughter have 15 girls over to spend the night?"

"What was I thinking when I agreed to make a meal for a sick friend, head up the Brownies meeting, and get my son to soccer—all at 5:30 P.M.?"

"What was I thinking when I accepted a date with Jim, who is not a Christian and who parties all the time?"

The list could go on and on. You may identify with some I included, or write your own. What were you thinking? Most likely you weren't thinking. You were reacting, responding to the emotional pull to make other people happy by doing what is on their agenda. It's time to think! If you are sure about your decision to begin living a life that matters, you are going to have to start thinking.

You'll be asked to stop and do some thinking in your journal exercise. Learn from your past by making a "What was I thinking?" list for yourself. Think about the last time you got yourself into an overcommitted mess, or an unhealthy relationship, or a wasted day. Yours could read: "What was I thinking when I sat and watched television for six hours, ate a whole bag of potato chips, and didn't call my friend or prepare for Bible study or play with my kids as I had planned?" Perhaps what you were thinking was, "I am depressed and need friends, but I'm afraid of rejection. I don't think I can take one more letdown or I might not be able to get up again." So sitting around all day avoiding your life was a result of fear.

Does that help you see how important your mind is to making meaningful changes? Real changes require real thoughtfulness, so here's some help for staying on top of things.

Organize Your Mind

Living a life that matters is about getting organized and confronting some of the pressures you unfairly put on yourself. I'm the worst at this, especially when I have a book deadline. If I let the thoughts in my head flow freely at times like these, they can overwhelm me to the point of despair. I confront them by getting organized. Other people may not be able to tell that I'm organized, but I can. I just take out my trusty legal pad and start categorizing the thoughts and pressures running through my mind. I list things I need to do for my church leadership, deadlines for my writing projects, what I need to do for the kids, and I assign dates for completing each task.

Organization saves you time and energy. Think of all the time and energy you use looking for things you need. If you could add it up over a lifetime, it might equal days or weeks—even years for some of us. Think about how much time you waste by forgetting important activities or walking around in a daze because you have so much to do that you don't know where to start. All of that wasted time is draining your energy, keeping you disappointed and dissatisfied with your life.

I don't know how any woman survives without a planner. The school my children attend puts out a notebook-sized planner for the school calendar year with preprinted dates relevant to the school. That planner remains in our kitchen and becomes the center of operations for our family. I also carry a purse-sized calendar with me, and for the electronically inclined, there are PDAs.

Getting organized starts with a plan. For example, your entire house may be in desperate need of organization, but you first have to do a little triage. Get out a legal pad and jot down areas in your life you need to organize: paying bills, managing the family calendar, cleaning house, cleaning closets, planning a women's retreat, or whatever. Then list what you need to do under each category. Next, prioritize. Beside each item write a deadline—dates by which you need to accomplish each item on your list. It makes sense to organize your family calendar and make a date with yourself to pay bills. One tip for saving time with bills is to use automatic deposit and bill payment if your bank offers this service.

But don't forget to stay on top of deposits and payments in your personal checkbook.

As much as possible, consolidate your errands so you don't waste time. Don't run out to do an errand the minute you think of it. Plan ahead and try to go to the dry cleaners, library, and video store the same day. You can train your family to let you know the things they need ahead of time, according to the day you run family errands. I keep a grocery list going in the kitchen. Everyone knows that the shopping will be done on Friday, so they had better plan ahead if they need more shampoo or whatever.

Start your day with an action plan; decide what is most important on your list and tackle it first. Otherwise you will listen to the loudest voice in your head, and it might lead you off track. For example, the thought that I should have my devotions is often the quietest. Once my kids are out of the house and on their way to school, I look around at the overflowing laundry, breakfast dishes, calendar full of projects, and the long to-do list. All these tasks seem to be calling out to me, demanding my attention. I have to make myself sit down in my living room, pick up my Bible and journal, and get connected to God. If I don't make myself take this time with God right then in the midst of all the chaos, I will try to squeeze it in later when I'm less open, or I will miss it all together. I can't rely on my immediate thoughts to judge what I should do each day. Instead, I use the priorities and principles that I have committed myself to as my guide.

Mind Your Money

One of the major energy drainers women deal with is concern about money. Many feel guilty about the way they manage their finances. Their minds are either focused on what they want to buy or how they can finagle paying for it. Peace of mind is robbed by an unbalanced checkbook or out-of-control spending.

Open your checkbook right now. Look at last month's checks. When was the last time you wrote a tithe (a 10 percent offering) to the church? If you are not giving a portion of your income to God, your checkbook is likely to be a mess no matter how much money you make.

Are you having a hard time deciding what to buy and what not to buy? Do you overspend, then wonder how you can make so much money yet be in a financial bind? Do you question how you could ever make enough money to meet your basic needs? Maybe you feel guilty and overwhelmed by the idea of giving to the church. I have been there myself.

I hate being in debt, yet several years ago Brian and I found ourselves with several thousands of dollars of credit card debt on top of our mortgage and car payments. We gave regularly to the church, but we weren't tithers. We didn't take our gross income and pay 10 percent of that as a weekly offering, but we felt it was time to change and we asked God to help. We began to tithe faithfully, Brian took a job that paid less, and we got out of debt.

I can't show you on paper exactly how it was that we got out of debt, but when we decided to give our 10 percent to the church, no matter what, we became much more thoughtful about how we spent what was left after taxes.

The Bible doesn't tell us that we cannot have debt, though it does have a lot to say about money, and giving, specifically. In Scripture there are 2,162 references to money. I have learned that people who are disciplined in giving are usually equally disciplined in money management. Giving to God with a humble and grateful heart is a spiritual discipline that accomplishes more spiritually for the giver than it does for the receiver.

In order to give regularly (such as a tithe), and give beyond that in certain situations, we must confront our own selfishness and materialism head-on. We all need to understand that everything we have is given to us by God. Don't claim your identity from your bank statement, but feel peace about your finances as you follow God's plan.

When your checkbook reflects God's values, you will have a life that is free of other vices. Managing your money well helps you be free of envy, materialism, and undisciplined spending. Most importantly, your life will demonstrate obedience to God. By-products of having God's perspective about money are: generosity, gratitude, contentment, and freedom from anxiety.

You may not realize how much an out-of-control checkbook is draining your energy. If your checkbook reveals that your life is a mess in this area, don't despair; get help. Two well-recognized Christian ministries that can help you learn to manage God's resources are Crown Financial Ministries and Ronald Blue & Co.[1] You can get started right now by praying over your checkbook and inviting God to give you His perspective about money. You can record each time you spend money and how you spent it. Carry a small notebook to make it easy to write down daily expenditures.

You need to see where you are spending your money before determining where to reorganize. When you set up a budget or plan for managing your money, include tithing, paying taxes, paying bills on time, saving, and a plan for getting out of debt, it will bring you peace of mind.

Guard Your Mind

It is essential that you guard your mind, to "think about the things you think about." What you let enter your mind affects you in ways you don't realize. The kind of entertainment you take in—TV, movies, conversations at parties, books you read—all of this affects your mind. I'm not recommending that you become a fanatic, or get overly anxious about your thoughts. I do recommend that you become aware of the pictures and thoughts entering your mind, and don't underestimate their impact.

Discover Your Mind

Computers are amazing inventions. I both hate and love them. I wrote my doctoral dissertation on a computer and I can't imagine how people wrote dissertations or books without them. The amazing thing about a computer is that it can put out only what has been input. You can't blame a computer for telling you that you misspelled *Thessalonians* if it hasn't been taught that it is a word. Your mind works the same way.

Sometimes your brain tells you that something you are doing is wrong, when actually it is right. Why? Because your brain hasn't learned the truth. Our brains absorb all kinds of information every day, and often we aren't even consciously aware of what is in there. Therefore, it's important for you to figure out how you figure.

What kinds of things are weighing heavily on your mind? Journal exercise #4 at the end of this chapter will help you determine if you are being plagued by thoughts you aren't aware of. Categories include your possessions, your body, your relationships, and your workload. If you discover an area that doesn't trouble you, give yourself a gold star and don't start obsessing over it.

Lisa's "What weighs on your mind?" exercise was very revealing. After she completed her exercise, she understood why she felt dismayed with her life. Lisa's possessions and workload worries left her little time to care about her relationships and her body. This made her think, *Maybe if I were more connected to my husband, we could work together on getting some of these things done.* Lisa realized that doing too much kept her from enjoying the people she was doing so much for.

Though Lisa's husband had been comfortable letting her worry about everything, he also welcomed the opportunity to work together. He was feeling lonely in their marriage. Lisa told her husband that all the issues she worried about kept her in a prison. He wanted to help her learn to slow down, worry less, and dream more.

Avoid Energy Drainers

How many issues are draining your mind and energy? No wonder you keep getting into those "What was I thinking?" situations. Second Corinthians 10:5 tells us to take every thought captive. You can learn how to use your mind to change your life, and the following steps can help you reach that goal:

1. Cleanse your mind. In counseling I have helped people recognize lies they believe that result in depression and anxiety. Some of these lies developed in childhood, yet they still create havoc today.

After 20 years of marriage, Charlene's husband finally convinced her to discuss her lack of sexual desire with a counselor. When we spoke, her face revealed the hopelessness she felt about the subject, as she recounted 20 years of marriage and enduring sex only because the Bible said she should. She confessed that she had never had much pleasure and wasn't even sure if she had ever had a climax in her life.

One of the lies that had affected her for 20 years was that sex is evil. Charlene was raised by very religious parents in a dysfunctional marriage; her father was controlling while her mother was weak and reserved. Charlene craved her father's attention and lost respect for her mother. The only time sex was ever mentioned in their house was by her father. He went on a tirade about boys and sex and how bad boyfriends were.

In counseling 20 years later, Charlene recounted those statements by her dad and realized how significant they were in her choice to shut down sexually. She believed the lie that sex was bad and that experiencing any sexual desires meant she was bad too. These lies had nearly destroyed her marriage.

Charlene is not alone. Many people believe lies about themselves based on unresolved childhood conflicts. You can guard your mind by understanding how the past may be tied to lies that are keeping you in bondage.

2. Deal with flaming arrows. Because of sin, it is much easier to think negatively than positively. Satan wants to use our minds against us. He knows how powerful the mind is over our feelings and actions. Those flaming arrows from the wicked one that we are warned about in Ephesians 6:16 are often negative thoughts that he puts in our minds. Again Paul gives you the key to defeating Satan's attempts at clouding your mind with negative content. In 2 Corinthians 10:4-5 we learn, "The weapons we fight with are not the weapons of the world. On the contrary, they have divine power to demolish strongholds. We demolish arguments and every pretension that sets itself up against the knowledge of God, and we take captive every thought to make it obedient to Christ."

Recognize that there is a battle for your mind. It takes effort and obedience to focus on God's truth. Your life may look like it is hopeless and worthless, but that's not true. You have to believe God's truth and put out those flaming arrows of negative thoughts.

3. Avoid negative input. Lynn could still recount the scenes of an X-rated movie she saw at age 14 while staying alone in her young adult brother's house. She found the video under his couch and knew it wasn't something she should watch, but she didn't stop herself. Now it only takes a moment to recall the graphic and disgusting images imprinted on her mind. She hates that she ever saw the movie and would never want to see it again. At age 38, those images are still a part of her mind, though she managed to escape pornography's addictive potential.

The things you put into your mind stay there. The old saying is true: garbage in, garbage out. How often have I watched some chick flick about relationship discord and violence that does me no good? I hate to think of all the negative things that enter my mind through television, movies, and radio. We all need to be aware of the power of the media that floods our minds daily.

4. Evaluate your self-talk. To change your habits or feelings, recognize that what you think influences your emotions, choices, and behavior. Consistent, long-term change will not happen if the mind hasn't been transformed. Are you feeling stuck? What is keeping you from focusing on the priorities God has set before you? What do you really think? Sometimes you may need God to expose your negative self-talk. What thoughts keep you from pursuing God's will for your life? In your journal, list any negative self-talk that comes to your mind right now.

Go back over your list and find scriptures that address each of the thoughts you mentioned. Here's an example of negative self-talk:

> God has called me to teach children's Sunday school, but I haven't even sent birthday cards to the kids in my class this year. I am a bad teacher. Rebuke: 2 Timothy 3:16-17 talks about teaching Scripture to help people live their lives for God. That is what I'm doing. I'm not going to let Satan, who is the accuser of the

brethren (Revelation 12:10), tell me that I am a bad teacher. I would like to think of a way I can organize myself to send birthday cards to the children in my class next year. But I refuse to think that I am a bad teacher.

You may need help from another Christian who knows God's Word when you are seeking His truth.

5. Meditate on God's Word. Philippians 4:8-9 says, "Finally, brothers, whatever is true, whatever is noble, whatever is right, whatever is pure, whatever is lovely, whatever is admirable—if anything is excellent or praiseworthy—think about such things. Whatever you have learned or received or heard from me, or seen in me—put it into practice. And the God of peace will be with you."

Do you need peace in your life? Study the Bible, and you'll find that meditating on God's Word affects your whole life. Meditating on God's Word means letting His Word penetrate your life. Take a passage such as the parable of the prodigal son in Luke 15:11-32. Meditate on it by asking yourself:
   • If I were the prodigal son, how would I feel?
   • Why would I want to leave my father?
   • If I were the father, why would I let my son go?
   • How would I feel toward my prodigal son and toward my elder son?
   • If I were the elder son, why wouldn't I join the celebration?
In this way you are actually personalizing Scripture. Many times when I meditate on Scripture, I find I have memorized it without intending to do so. Meditating on Scripture requires slowly reading it and letting it sink into you, allowing the Holy Spirit to give you personal insights about the mystery of God. This practice of letting God's Word become a part of you can give you the wisdom to correct your negative self-talk, ward off Satan's flaming arrows, cleanse you from past hurts, and help you recognize negative input.

6. Give yourself permission. There are areas in which we need to give ourselves permission if we are going to be free to make the necessary changes in our lives. You need to give yourself permission to believe that your life is important and special to God. You need to give yourself permission to say no. You need to give yourself permission to consider your own needs, as well as those of your family. You need to give yourself permission to accept your less-than-perfect body and permission to be seen without makeup.

However, some things that weigh heavily on our hearts and minds don't need to be there because we shouldn't give ourselves permission to dwell on them. These may include permission to consider divorce as a way out of our marriage, permission to consider thoughts of suicide, or even permission to be cranky and moody.

You can see how closely connected the truth of the Spirit is to having a healthy mind-set. In the next chapter we'll consider how much a healthy mind benefits healthy emotions.

Journal Exercises

1. What would it take to get organized? Follow the steps to organizing your life on pages 92-93; make your list in your journal.
2. If you don't have a budget, make one this week.
3. "What was I thinking?" exercise:
    - Think back to the last time you got into an overcommitted mess. Finish this sentence about that event: "What was I thinking when . . ."
    - Describe the mess.
    - Describe why you think you really allowed that to happen.
4. "What weighs on your mind?" exercise:
    - What weighs on your mind about the things you possess?
      -wardrobe
      -car
      -house/apartment
      -how your home is decorated
      -appliances
      -clutter
      -other home repairs

-messy house

-personal financial pressures

-balancing the checkbook

-paying the bills

-other

• What weighs on your mind about you and your body?

-how you look

-unread books

-sleep

-exercise

-regular doctor or dentist appointments

-eating habits

-health concerns for yourself

-need for something in your life

-lack of time with God

-other

• What weighs on your mind about your relationships?

-someone is angry with you

-someone has disappointed you

-you know you need to disappoint someone

-child with special problems

-marital conflict

-in-law conflict

-issues with the family you grew up in

-balancing time with friends

-other

• What weighs you down from your workload? (Stay-at-home work or outside employment plus the stress at home)

-stressful days

-tedious work responsibilities

-lack of appropriate information to complete task

-lack of help needed to complete task

-disorganization of personnel or environment

-difficult relationships

-being taken advantage of by others' lack of responsibility

-overloaded with impossible responsibilities
-church responsibilities
-other

Goal for the Week

Don't answer yes to any request this week. Tell the person you will get back to him or her, then take time to pray before you give your answer.

Chapter Nine

Making Over Your Emotions

Therefore we do not lose heart. Though outwardly
we are wasting away, yet inwardly we are being renewed
day by day. For our light and momentary troubles are
achieving for us an eternal glory that far outweighs
them all. So we fix our eyes not on what is seen,
but on what is unseen. For what is seen is temporary,
but what is unseen is eternal.

2 CORINTHIANS 4:16-18

Cynthia is curled up into a ball in her closet crying hysterically. Her children keep coming to the door to peek in on her. She knows they are out there, but she doesn't know how to stop crying, get up, and reassure them that everything is okay. She wants to do that, but she feels she has gone to a place from which there is no return, and she isn't sure how she got there.

This episode was triggered after Cynthia had walked into the family room to find mud spread on the walls, carpet, and furniture. The kids had let their two Labrador retrievers into the house while she was on the phone. When the kids saw that the dogs were muddy, they chased them all around the room trying to shoo them back out, but not before the dogs had spread muddy paw prints everywhere.

Maybe Cynthia could have handled it if her whole day hadn't consisted of running from one mess to another. She just couldn't manage one more thing. When she walked into the room and discovered the mess, she screamed in a tone she'd never used before and slowly walked away. She ended up on the floor of her closet, curled up in a ball and crying like a baby. How did that happen?

Cynthia's emotional meltdown occurred because she hadn't been taking care of her emotional self throughout the day (and in her case probably for weeks and months). Finally her emotions just took over. To avoid emotional meltdowns like this, it is important to be able to identify and resolve your emotions when they occur.

What are you feeling right now? Take a moment and get connected to your feelings. Is it hard? Or do you know what you are feeling immediately? For some women, getting in touch with their genuine feelings is difficult. Others are very aware of their feelings but don't know what to do with them.

Women are generally known for their emotional nature. Most of us aren't ashamed to cry at commercials. We are open to expressing love and appreciation for others. We feel deep connections to others through emotional bonding. Women can also be bothered by their emotions. If you don't know how to deal with your emotions, they can create crises in your life.

How to Control Your Emotions

You do not have direct control over your emotions. How's that for an answer? The truth is that you don't have *direct* control over your emotions, but you do have *indirect* control. The indirect control stems from what you think.

Albert Ellis is famous for his A+B=C theory. In his theory, A is the event, C is the emotional response to the event, and B is the belief about the event. He illustrates this with a scenario about seeing a bear. The same event (A) seeing a bear can cause different emotions (C) depending on what the person who sees the bear believes (B) about the event of seeing a bear. For example, if you see the bear in the woods and it is coming toward you to attack, your feeling (C) would be fear. But, if you see the bear at the zoo, safely behind bars, your feeling (C) might be pleasure in seeing such a cute bear.

Thinking about the truth (renewing your mind, Romans 12:1) will result in emotional responses that are appropriate and don't feel out of control. Notice that the result isn't necessarily pleasurable feelings. We all want to feel good all the time, but in a sinful world we have to create space for negative feelings. Some women need the courage to feel bad feelings.

In counseling I meet women with full-fledged anxiety disorders. They have developed these disorders because they don't let themselves experience their negative feelings. For instance, a woman might be angry about a pregnancy that ended in miscarriage, but her spirituality won't allow her to admit that she's angry. She represses the anger and eventually develops irrational fears and anxiety or depression.

It is vital to mental health to learn how to fully acknowledge your emotions, recognizing emotions as friends instead of enemies and making choices about the best way to express your feelings.

You have numerous emotional reactions each day because you are created in God's likeness, and God is an emotional being. Fortunately, God does not express each emotion fully. God is angry about sin, but He has delayed expressing His full wrath against sin. Revelation 6:15-17 foretells the response of the inhabitants of the earth when the righteous wrath of God will at last be released. Thankfully, God gives everyone an opportunity to avoid His wrath before He expresses it.

Exercises for Emotional Health

Emotions function a lot like the warning lights in our cars. Usually when the light comes on it doesn't mean that your car is going to break down in the next five minutes. However, it does mean that you need to get a mechanic to check out what's wrong.

I'm one of those stereotypical women who don't pay much attention to those silly lights on the dashboard. My husband is baffled by the fact that one of those lights might be on for days and I'll keep forgetting to tell him about it. (Actually, after a cracked engine block early in our marriage, I have gotten a lot better about tuning in to any warning lights in my car.)

Though I might be tempted to ignore the dashboard warning lights, I don't ignore my emotions. Emotions are often our first clue that something needs attention in our lives. When you have a new feeling, you need to consider what it reveals about what's going on in your life.

Don't judge your emotions as good or bad, but see them as signals that alert you to pay attention to events. Many women become emotionally crippled because they are so worried about what others might think of them if they show anger.

Bad Feelings Can Be Good for You!

Most of us focus our emotional energy on avoiding so-called bad feelings. We don't like to feel mad, hurt, or depressed, but unless we acknowledge those "bad" feelings, we can never experience peace. Romans 8:6 says that the mind controlled by the Spirit leads to life and deeper peace. Therefore, we need the Spirit's mind about our emotions; we can't get deeper peace by avoiding our feelings.

Janet constantly finds herself angry with her mother because she can't have one conversation in which Mom doesn't mention Janet's brother's children and how perfect and wonderful they are. Janet hates seeing herself as needy and jealous of her brother, Gary. After all, she has a relationship with God and he doesn't. She doesn't like having to admit that she is being petty. She feels ashamed about the reality of her feelings, and that shame keeps her from receiving emotional peace.

Janet is troubled by two negative emotions. She is not only angry with her mother, she also feels ashamed of herself. After all, she reminds herself, *I am a Christian, and Mom and Gary are not.* Her shame stems from the fact that she tries to be the perfect Christian in front of them. If she represses these feelings, she will end up setting herself up for anxiety or depression, and if she expresses them freely, she is likely to blow up at her mother and shed a poor light on Christ. What can she do? Here are some ways to deal with negative emotions.

1. Always acknowledge your emotion. The first thing Janet needs to do is fully acknowledge her feelings. She needs to allow herself to see the dark realities of her heart, which she doesn't like to acknowledge. It would be most helpful to admit these feelings to herself and God, and if she has someone who can support her and guide her to truth about them, to confess to that person as well.

What emotion is troubling you right now? Is it anger, jealousy, fear, sadness, irritation? Your emotions are God-given. Some Christians won't let themselves admit they have anger, hurt, or other negative emotions because they think it is unspiritual. However, repressing your emotions can lead to depression, anxiety, and stress, so seek to fully admit your emotions to God and yourself. God already knows what you're feeling, so He won't be shocked when you admit it.

I find it helpful to journal about my emotions—especially the negative ones. If you don't like writing, you could go to a room by yourself and speak out your emotions—cry, shout, tell God what you honestly feel!

2. Discover what beliefs are causing the emotion. Janet found that her anger was based on her need to be treated equally with her brother, a feeling she'd had all her life. She asked herself, *Why do I need to be equal to him? If I didn't have that need to be equal to Gary in every way, I could save myself a lot of emotional pain. Mom is not very likely to change after all these years. Just because she doesn't brag about my children doesn't make them any less wonderful. Mom doesn't have to see my children the way I do.*

Just looking at her belief system brought relief to the pain Janet was feeling. But what could she do about the emotional strain? She needed an outlet for the anger she felt.

3. Evaluate your belief in light of God's Word. Once you figure out what beliefs trigger the negative emotions, you need to evaluate whether your beliefs are true or not. It is helpful to have someone with whom you can check out the beliefs underneath your feelings. You need someone who will be honest with you and who is willing to confront you when you are wrong.

We have been promised a Counselor who is eager to be called on 24 hours a day. He is always interested in talking to you and definitely willing to show you the truth. It is the Holy Spirit (John 16:13). With the Holy Spirit and God's Word, you can connect your feelings and beliefs to His truth. Try humbly coming before God with your negative emotions and ask Him to direct you from His Word. Here are some places you can start.

- When Angry: Ephesians 4:26-27, Proverbs 16:32, Colossians 3:8, Nahum 1:3
- When Anxious: Philippians 4:6-7, Romans 8:15, 2 Timothy 1:7, Psalm 27:1, Proverbs 3:25
- When Jealous: 1 Timothy 6:4, Proverbs 23:17, Proverbs 27:4, Romans 13:12, 14
- When Depressed: Psalm 42:5-6, Psalm 69:13, Job 1:1, Genesis 48:11, Isaiah 22:12-13
- When Bitter: James 2:5, 1 John 3:15, Hebrews 12:16, Luke 15:30, Philippians 1:12-14, Genesis 33:1-11
- When Hating Others: Exodus 11:9-10, Psalm 95:8, Psalm 95:11, Jeremiah 4:3, Romans 11:8-9, 1 John 4:19
- When Feeling Inferior: Galatians 3:5, Mark 9:34, 1 Samuel 9:21
- When Sad: Luke 24:51, Mark 1:2-3, Isaiah 40:1-2, Job 16:1
- When Hopeless: Mark 5:35-36, Luke 18:35, 2 Corinthians 4:18, 1 Corinthians 15:54-56, Philippians 3:13-14
- When Disappointed: James 4:13-16, Philippians 1:12-14, Nehemiah 4:10-14, Nehemiah 4:1-5
- When Judgmental of Others: Matthew 7:1, Romans 14:10-12, Acts 11:2-18, Isaiah 11:3-5

Janet was reading 1 Timothy 6 in her devotions. The Holy Spirit seemed to shout to her in verse 4, "He is conceited and understands nothing. He has an unhealthy interest in controversies and quarrels about words that result in envy, strife, malicious talk, evil suspicions...." Though this verse was describing false teachers, Janet found it revealed her inner flaw. She was jealous because she lacked understanding. Whenever she lost touch with the reality that she is God's daughter— loved unreservedly—she tried to cling to her mother for a love her mother could not give and became jealous of her brother for seeming to have the love she wants. Suddenly, she realized what she was doing and how unfounded her beliefs about her family were.

4. Think through the best way to express your emotion. Coming to God and His Word gave Janet the power to totally turn her anger around. Rather than express her anger at her mother, Janet expressed her anger to God. Along with telling Him how angry and hurt she was, she confessed how petty she felt for getting so upset by such a small incident. She told Him she was powerless to get over her anger on her own, and she asked for His help.

She felt God comforting her as she read about Jesus' anguish that God appeared to have abandoned Him (Matthew 27:46). She knew she had a High Priest who could identify with her hurt, because deep down she did feel forsaken by her mother for favoring her brother. This insight brought her peace. The hurt, which was deeper than her anger, was healed by God's comfort. His acknowledgment and response to her pain took away shame and brought a deeper connection to Him.

She found a new strength to forgive her mother for being human, and for not being able to see her positive qualities as a daughter. She didn't need her mother's approval as much anymore because God's approval was more powerful. With the Spirit's help, she recognized how sharing her feelings with her mother might improve their relationship. She decided to reveal that she felt a little hurt that her mother didn't seem to think as highly of her children as Gary's.

The next time they talked, Janet told her mother about her true feelings. She didn't make accusations but explained that she got off the phone wondering if her mother thought as highly about her children. Janet's mother was taken aback at first and tried to deny expressing any preference. Janet accepted this and continued the conversation in a loving manner. Janet didn't think anything would change between them, but she noticed over time that her mother was more interested in her children and knowing what they were doing.

One day, her mother confessed, "I think I talked about Gary's children so much because I thought you thought you were perfect because you go to church and I guess I felt a little defensive."

Janet responded with understanding. She apologized for giving the impression that she was better than her mother or her brother because she was a Christian. The conversation provided the first opportunity Janet ever had to share the gospel with her mother. Janet's honesty about her emotions and her weakness became the catalyst for opening her mother's mind and spirit to what Janet had found in Christ.

How Hormones Affect Emotions

Research shows that hormonal changes do affect women's emotional responses. During phases of your cycle, your estrogen will be elevated. This may result in an increase in anger, anxiety, depression, and so on. It is very important to discuss this with your physician. The advice given here about managing emotions can be used as well, but you may have chemical changes in your body that make managing your emotions more difficult.

There are plenty of jokes that go around addressing a woman's emotional ups and downs. My husband sent me this e-mail recently:

Hormone Hostage Handbook for Husbands, Boyfriends, and Significant Others

(Source unknown, or unwilling to identify himself)

What to Say When . . .

Dangerous: What's for dinner?

Safer: Can I help you with dinner?

Safest: Where would you like to go for dinner?

Dangerous: Are you wearing that?

Safer: Gee, you look good in brown.

Safest: WOW! Look at you!

Dangerous: What did you do all day?

Safer: I hope you didn't overdo it today.

Safest: I've always loved you in that robe.

All kidding aside, hormones can sometimes interfere with emotional well-being. As we seek to live lives that matter, we shouldn't make things harder for ourselves by ignoring our complicated chemical makeup.

As Cassie has gotten older, she has noticed that her feelings of anger have become more pronounced; her outbursts at her husband and children have become more explosive and frequent. She doesn't like this about herself, but the more effort she puts into suppressing her anger, the angrier she gets. She feels completely out of control. What can she do?

Cassie is a classic example of a woman whose chemical changes have affected her emotional well-being. She can't attribute all of her increased anger to hormones (like everyone, she has a sin nature), but a doctor's blood test revealed the frequency and intensity of her anger was likely due to a hormonal imbalance. The doctor prescribed hormones, and three months later both she and her family saw a dramatic decrease in her angry outbursts.

If you suspect that your emotional fluctuations are a result of hormonal issues and for health or other reasons are not able to take medication, there are other options. Chart your cycle on a calendar and be prepared for your more difficult days. For instance, don't plan a party at your house when you know you won't be chemically at your best. When you can't stop the world for your cycle, plan for support to get you through your hard times. Acknowledging the reason for your tenseness can be extremely helpful in dissipating its power over you.

Other Physical Factors

Hormones aren't the only chemicals that affect mood. Not getting proper rest, exercise, and food will create havoc with your emotions. Chapter seven addressed these issues. Taking care of your body has a benefit in addition to providing the energy you need to live your life—you also gain the advantage of more stable moods.

Dealing with Others' Emotions

Besides mishandling their own emotions, some women are compelled to take responsibility for others' emotions. We feel it is our job to make our husbands happy, to keep our kids satisfied, and to avoid disappointing anyone. The age-old saying, "If Mama ain't happy, ain't nobody happy," could be reversed: "If everyone ain't happy, Mama ain't happy." Do you often feel at fault when someone close to you experiences negative emotions?

You can't change other people's emotions and you are not responsible for the emotional reactions of others. This is very hard for women to grasp. We need to learn how to accept that when someone we love is sad or mad, it is that person's problem, not ours. If someone tells you he or she is angry because of something you did, listen and respond appropriately. But too many women try to control the feelings of others without letting others be responsible for themselves. This is damaging to the woman as well as those whose feelings she is trying to resolve.

Remember: You can be a sounding board. You can offer advice and support. But you are not responsible for how others feel.

Hebrews 12:14 says, "Make every effort to live at peace with all men." Living at peace with everyone is not totally under our control. God knows this, and that is why He doesn't direct us to have peace in all of our relationships, but rather tells us to do everything we can do to promote peace. Emotional wholeness is good for the spirit; it brings peace to the core of your life. Though emotional wholeness is not achieved without struggle, it is well worth pursuing as it leads to deeper peace.

Journal Exercise

Follow these steps to emotional health:

1. Always acknowledge your emotions. What negative feeling do you have right now? What is the last negative feeling you can remember? Write it down and describe how you experienced it.
2. Evaluate the things you believe about yourself and others which may be causing this emotion.
3. Evaluate your belief. All beliefs are real, but not all beliefs are true. Is your belief consistent with God's Word? (Use the scriptures provided in this chapter for help, or call someone with spiritual maturity to guide you.)

4. Think through the best way to express your emotion. If in step three you realized your feelings were unfounded, the feelings will be resolved. But if your feelings are based on truth, determine the best way to express them. Ephesians 4:26 tells us not to sin in our anger. Your negative emotions are not sin, but your choices about expressing anger and other negative emotions can be sinful. How can you best express your negative emotion without sinning?

Repeat this exercise for every emotion you have until it becomes an automatic response.

Goal for the Week

Every time you acknowledge your emotion, make yourself smile (even if it is a negative emotion) and thank God for making you an emotional being.

Chapter Ten

Making Over Your Spirit

Devote yourselves to prayer, being watchful and thankful.
COLOSSIANS 4:2

I wouldn't exactly categorize myself as directionally challenged, but I am surprised at how easily I can lose my way. My daughter helps me get back on track, especially in downtown Dallas where I have to drive her to doctor's appointments. I don't understand how I can make the same mistakes, or why I can't easily find my way each time, but something goes wrong and I don't see the right road until it's too late. Then I have to navigate with God's help (I've learned to drive and pray at the same time), listening to my daughter's suggestions. I usually get us home by dinnertime.

It's the same with my spiritual life. I've got the directions down. In fact, Jesus summarized them for me: Love God and love others (Matthew 22:34-40). That's not too complicated. If I were asked to take a written test, I know I could pass. But executing it is a different story. It's easy to describe the kind of life I want to live and the priorities I want to have, but it is altogether different to make those things happen each day.

To live a life that matters I have to stay spiritually centered. Without Christ at the center of my life, I'm without hope altogether. I'll never get it right on my own. In Philippians 4:13 the apostle Paul writes, "I can do everything through him who gives me strength." That could also be stated, "I can't do a thing to live my life right if I don't rely on God who gives me strength."

Let's explore some exercises that will keep you relying on God to center your life and your activities.

MAKE YOUR SPIRIT A PRIORITY

You are a spiritual being. The spiritual part of you distinguishes you from God's other creations. After God created Adam from the dust, He breathed His Spirit into him (Genesis 2:7).

Our modern world tries to ignore the fact that we are spiritual beings. Many people in the 1970s and 1980s focused on pleasure and work. This led many to a spiritual reawakening by the turn of the century. Unfortunately, most people aren't seeking the true Spirit but are trying to address their spirituality outside of the context of God. Living a life that matters involves addressing your spirituality and finding ways to allow your spirit to connect to God and energize you. If you do not tend to your spiritual life, it will atrophy.

Despite our best efforts, most of us fail to make tending our spirits a priority. Often, we don't think about our spirits until we have stressed ourselves to the point of exhaustion. Then we desperately pray for help.

Too many faithful church attendees never worship in their place of worship. Rather, they spend their hours at church teaching children, making meals, or performing acts of service, and they never connect their duties to worship. Jesus said, "Yet a time is coming and has now come when the true worshipers will worship the Father in spirit and truth, for they are the kind of worshipers the Father seeks" (John 4:23). God isn't interested in how many praise songs you know. He doesn't care how many hymns you can sing without using the hymnbook. He does care about the spiritual connection you make to Him. He doesn't want to connect to you only in church worship; He wants you to worship Him every day and every moment of every day.

Brother Lawrence is known for living the kind of life that connects to God. I encourage you to read *The Practice of the Presence of God*,[1] a compilation of letters he wrote during his 25 years of service in the community of believers. Brother Lawrence lived in France in the 1600s, and worked in a hospital kitchen. He insisted that fully devoting himself to God could be accomplished in the context of his ordinary life. In other words, he didn't feel that devout believers had to live in a monastery to dedicate their lives to God. He wrote, "In fact, I'd go so far as to say that the very best way of coming closer to God that I have yet discovered—far better than those dreary mechanical devotions recommended by some of the textbooks—is to do my ordinary, everyday business without any view of pleasing people, but as far as I can, purely for the love of God."[2]

He prescribes this exercise to a soldier who had written to him: "Think of God as often as you can, and especially in times of danger. Just a little lifting up of the heart is enough—a little remembrance of God, a brief act of inward worship—even out on patrol, or on guard with a rifle in your hands: God hears and understands. He is near, and you will know it."[3]

The mistake we often make is to categorize our lives into sacred and secular activities. This is not the way God made us. We need to be the integrated creations that God brilliantly designed; otherwise, we will give up on living meaningful lives and conform to doing only what is necessary. How do you tend your spirit and still finish the laundry?

Think about it: Laundry is one of those tasks almost everybody has to do. It never stops. Even if you have every piece of dirty clothing in your entire house laundered, you are still wearing clothes that are getting dirtier by the minute. There is never a moment completely free of all laundry. Doing laundry and tending to your spirit have something in common. Both are continual quests, and you never completely finish either.

Doing the laundry can become a spiritual task as you pray for each person whose clothes you are folding, as you thank God for the strength to do the work, as you become thankful for all the clothes you are blessed to own.

Tending Your Spirit Requires Discipline

Practicing spiritual disciplines is one of the most rewarding efforts I make in life, but even though it's rewarding, it still requires discipline. I often have to make myself spend time with God. God promises that His Word will not return void (Isaiah 55:11), and I have found that promise to be true over and over in my life.

When you do physical exercise, it's important to set higher goals for yourself. After all, you don't want to stay in the same place for years. It is the same with spiritual discipline. The only difference is you never get too old or wear out your joints when you practice spiritual discipline— you just get stronger and better.

Candy decided to read through the Bible in one year. This seemed like a lofty task for her because she had never considered herself the intense Bible-reading type. She saw that as something a Sunday school teacher or minister would do. It was hard work. Sometimes she missed her daily reading and then she'd have to catch up. Other days she read the Bible like the newspaper, getting information only, with little that personally related to her life. But by the end of the year, she noticed something surprising. Through her Bible reading Candy was actually beginning to sense God's presence. There were times that her Bible reading actually gave her wisdom for dealing with anger at her husband or words to share with a friend. Even with such positive results, she still found it hard some days to resist turning on the morning news and open her Bible instead.

You might think tending to your spirit is something you will automatically do because it makes you feel so good. Think again. You won't always be eager to practice the disciplines that are necessary to tend your spirit. Sometimes you will want to do anything but read your Bible or pray. Don't be alarmed; it's because of your sin nature. God understands it. He knows that you are weak (1 Corinthians 1:27).

The only way to get stronger is to discipline yourself to meet with God in His Word. I encourage people to start with just 10 minutes. You can find 10 minutes in any day if you make it a priority. It's not about the number of minutes or hours you spend with God, it is about the openness of your spirit to receive.

Tending Your Spirit Has Eternal Significance

The physical discipline we endure on this earth gives our bodies energy for each day. The spiritual discipline we develop affects our spirits for eternity. Isn't that good motivation for tending your spirit? Paul reasons, "Everyone who competes in the games goes into strict training. They do it to get a crown that will not last; but we do it to get a crown that will last forever" (1 Corinthians 9:25).

Isn't that what living a life that matters is all about—focusing on a life that will count for eternity? Don't you want to be a shrewd manager of the life you have been given?

Tending Your Spirit Will Result in Christlikeness

You are seeking a life that matters because you would like to have all this life offers you and be the best person you can be. The absolute best description of the person you want to be is found in 2 Corinthians 3:18: "And we, who with unveiled faces all reflect the Lord's glory, are being transformed into his likeness with ever-increasing glory, which comes from the Lord, who is the Spirit." Being the person you want to be happens as you spend time in God's Word, yielding to His Spirit. When this occurs, you are transformed; others notice the glory that comes from you. There's no other place to find that glory than from God's Spirit.

St. Augustine made this observation:

> But just as God does not dwell within everyone, so he does not equally fill everyone in whom he does dwell. Otherwise, why should Elisha pray twice for the Spirit of God to be in him that was in Elijah? And how else can we explain that some Christians are clearly holier than others, unless God is dwelling more completely in them?
>
> This raises a further question. If God is wholly present everywhere in his creation, how can it be that he is more or less present in some of his creatures (and not present in some of them at all)?
>
> The answer lies in the capacity of things to receive him, not in his willingness to fill them.[4]

Christlikeness may seem a high and lofty goal, but it is the goal. Sometimes I wonder how God could come up with a plan like that for me. I fall so short of Christlikeness. Yet, it is God's plan. God has predestined me to be conformed to the image of Christ (Romans 8:29). When we see Him, we will be like Him (1 John 3:2). Deep in your spirit you long to love God and others like Jesus did. When we are loving others in Christ, it is the greatest experience of earthly existence. Nothing can compare to the immense excitement of being deeply connected to God through Christ.

Tending Your Spirit Requires Focus

Just as the early church discovered, it is easy to try to meet your spiritual needs without God. In Galatians 3:3 Paul warns, "Are you so foolish? After beginning with the Spirit, are you now trying to attain your goal by human effort?" It is often hard for us to do things in the Spirit. We might begin in the Spirit, but soon we resort to human effort.

I'm thankful for the ways God consistently lets me fall flat on my face when I am trying to do His work by myself. It is His love that lets me fail. He wants me to come to Him and learn how to glorify Him. I can't do this on my own. I'm not saying that I learn that lesson easily or triumphantly all the time, but I'm grateful that He does allow me to fail in my own strength. I've never experienced more spiritual victory than when I am conscious of my weakness.

The first step of Alcoholics Anonymous is to say, "I admit that I am powerless." That's the first step of spiritual growth as well. You have to keep yourself in check, recognizing when you are striving for spirituality by human effort. Once you recognize that, your prayer becomes, "God, I am powerless to (lead worship/do this project/love my husband). Please use me to glorify You."

If you are like me, you will find that you constantly have to refocus even after you've experienced total reliance on Him. It's so natural and easy for human beings to think of the things we can do and the effort we can make. I even find myself claiming God's spiritual gifts to me as my own gifts from time to time. Our battle to see the truth of life is constant, but it is fruitful when we fully give ourselves through discipline and focus.

Tending Your Spirit Produces Fruit

Who doesn't want more love, joy, peace, patience, kindness, goodness, faithfulness, gentleness, and self-control (Galatians 5:22-23)? Consistently abiding in the vine (Jesus Christ) will produce that kind of fruit in your life. Real love, joy, peace, etc. will not be achieved through human effort. Don't decide that you are going to make yourself more loving, joyful, peaceful, patient. If you long for these fruits, then long for God. The more time you spend in the presence of God, the more you will see these fruits in your life. They are by-products of tending your spirit. You can actually judge the results of the discipline and focus you have been giving to your spirit by the evidence of these characteristics in your life.

Others may recognize the changes in you before you do yourself. Your kids might say, "Mommy, you don't get as mad as you used to." (That's patience.) Your best friend might point out, "You're not getting as impatient with other drivers." (That's self-control.) You might be the one to recognize that you are sharing in ministry not to be noticed or valued in the church, but purely out of your love for and obedience to Christ. As you are tending your spirit, watch for these fruits in your life.

Spiritual Disciplines to Practice

1. Meditating on God's Word. There is no replacement for the Word of God when tending your spirit. It is the root of spiritual growth, and it provides the nutrients for your spirit's needs. It protects from disease. John 1:1 says, "In the beginning was the Word, and the Word was with God, and the Word was God." Then verse 14 goes on to explain, "The Word became flesh and made his dwelling among us. We have seen his glory, the glory of the One and Only, who came from the Father, full of grace and truth."

Now that's powerful. It helps us recognize the power of the Word in our lives. Your spirit will never grow unless you commit yourself to reading the Word.

2. Prayer. Prayer is the most amazing privilege known to man. Can you imagine that we are invited to casually, formally, in the swells of anxiety, at a moment of disaster, anytime, anywhere, or in any place, talk to God? What would it be like for you if you could just call the president of the United States anytime you wanted to and receive his full attention? You could call him just to say, "Hi." You could call and get an instant connection the exact moment you see a car headed toward you. It seems absurd doesn't it? And it is absurd. What could the president of the United States do for you or say to you at times like that? He could never be there for you the way you need him to be.

In prayer, you and I are not only invited, but we are encouraged to come. In fact, there is nothing that delights God more than for His children to come to Him in prayer. In true prayer, there is a two-way conversation. Most of us get bored with prayer because we pray like we are reciting a grocery list. Please give me this, and protect me from that, and this, and that, and the other. It gets monotonous. When we start listening in prayer and hearing the Spirit give us wisdom, guidance, and inspiration, prayer takes on a whole new dimension.

3. Fasting. Many religions enforce specific times for fasting. Most Christian denominations view fasting as a sign of total reliance on God and devotion to Him. I've grown to appreciate the spiritual marvel of fasting because in my experience, fasting has produced a spiritual strength in me that I can't explain.

4. Forgiveness. Forgiveness needs to be a daily discipline. There is always one person who will cross your path and leave behind some bitter feeling. I have met so many people who can't enjoy mental, spiritual, and physical health because of unforgiveness. Lack of forgiveness can lead to profound problems in life. I often give this exercise written by Miriam Pollard to individuals who need to focus on forgiving someone.

Is there someone you need to forgive? Try following these four steps to praying for that person. You will need about 30 minutes and a quiet place to be with God.

1. Praise God for all the beauty in the person, for all the defects, suffering, and moral lapses of his life. Praise God because all the inadequate and painful elements we see are hiding places for the loving work of God, bringing this member of Christ's body to happiness and goodness in a way we can't see. This is a very restful prayer.

2. Sink into God's love for the other, who is enfolded in this horizonless, infinite love. Love this person with God's own love.

3. Place yourself within the person, in quiet attentiveness before God. Ask healing and opening from within the other's need.

4. Ask God how you may improve your relationship with this person. Ask forgiveness for anything you have done to spoil it.[5]

When you experience forgiving another person through God's power, it is a life-changing experience. You are never the same thereafter. You are transformed from being a bitter, angry, wounded woman, to someone who is freed from the prison of hatred and obsession.

5. Giving. God loves a cheerful giver (2 Corinthians 9:7). Our spirits are nurtured through giving. We can give of our money, our time, and our talent. When we give to others we reveal the image of God. Henri Nouwen wrote, "I believe that, beyond all our desires to be appreciated, rewarded and acknowledged, there lies a simple and pure desire to give."[6]

Giving is one of the spiritual disciplines that we assume has the least benefit to our own lives. That is simply not true. When I am using my resources (money, talents, time) to help others, I am happiest. Rather than using everything I have on myself and feeling empty, when I give what I have to others I feel useful and satisfied. Giving is a huge benefit to my spirit and my soul.

6. Saying no to the sin nature. Romans 13:12-14 gives this advice: "The night is nearly over; the day is almost here. So let us put aside the deeds of darkness and put on the armor of light. Let us behave decently, as in the daytime, not in orgies and drunkenness, not in sexual immorality and debauchery, not in dissension and jealousy. Rather, clothe yourselves with the Lord Jesus Christ, and do not think about how to gratify the desires of the sinful nature." Tending your spirit means doing the opposite of what your sinful nature entices you to do. There is a constant battle within you to fulfill the desires of the Spirit rather than the sinful nature. You must be aware of this battle every day and your obligation to live by the Spirit (see Romans 8:12).

You build up your spirit when you say no to your sinful nature. You feed the Spirit when you turn off the television and have your devotions.

7. Devotional reading. The thoughts of Christians who have been dead for centuries have inspired me more than many Christians I have met personally. I'm amazed at how many years and differences separate me from their lives and circumstances, yet their insights into the soul still relate to my life.

Joan Chittister comments on one of the rules of St. Benedict: "I suddenly realized one morning in chapel at the daily oral reading of the Rule that Benedict wasn't saying that someone should be sent around the monastery to see if people were doing their work. He was saying that they should be sent around the monastery to see if the monastics were doing their reading and reflecting. The community should be mindful, in other words, to see that people were taking time to have a thoughtful as well as productive life."[7] St. Benedict put great importance on the need to be inspired by others along the spiritual journey. Daily inspiration is invaluable to living a life well.

8. Sabbath rest. If I were to make a list of the top 10 ways I energize my soul, number one would be to practice Sabbath rest on Sunday. Sabbath rest for me is defined as not doing anything on my to-do list. Instead I can choose to play basketball with my son, take a walk with my husband, read a book, take a hot bath, or even go shopping with my daughter.

This is where our souls get energized. Americans are go-getters, workers, and we apply this same approach to our Christian lives. It feels better to be chasing, dreaming, or running after something than to be sitting, enjoying being in the world. Yet soulful rest gives us the energy we need and is a key to healthy living.

God created us with physical needs that help us rely on Him. Jesus taught us to pray, "Give us each day our daily bread" (Luke 11:3), and we recognize that our physical needs bring us to dependence on God. Exercising your spirit is where you find the deepest meaning and purpose in life. The spirit inside you is the source of discerning what is really important in this world and helping you stay on track for living a life that matters.

Journal Exercise

1. For the next three Sundays, commit to Sabbath rest.
2. In what ways have you tended your spirit this week?
3. Remember the time you felt most alive in your spirit. Where were you? What were the circumstances?
4. How can you tend your spirit every day?
5. What can you do to make tending your spirit a priority?
6. What spiritual disciplines are you practicing? Which ones can you develop more? Make spiritual goals for yourself in the following areas:
   - meditating on God's Word
   - prayer
   - fasting
   - forgiveness
   - giving
   - saying no to the sin nature
   - devotional reading
   - other

Goal for the Week

Make a note each time you say no to the sin nature and picture Satan defeated.

Chapter Eleven

Relationships Get in the Way

*Speak and act as those who are going to be judged by the
law that gives freedom, because judgment without mercy
will be shown to anyone who has not been merciful.
Mercy triumphs over judgment!*
JAMES 2:12-13

❂

*L*iving a life that matters may involve straightening out your relationships. Remember Emma, the overwhelmed mother and
friend whose relationships were the source of much stress in her life?
Emma felt sorry for her friend Jane, never wanting to hurt her because
Jane had so many problems. Emma thought she could help Jane by
never requiring anything from their friendship. Though this seemed
noble on Emma's part, it didn't allow Jane to be the friend that Emma
needed at times.

Like Emma, you need to identify whether you are involved in draining relationships and what you can do to change them. Relationships
require energy. Now, I'm not proposing that you get rid of all the friends
who don't build you up. I am suggesting, however, that you think about
your relationships and how they relate to your goal of living a life that
pleases God. Do some of your relationships keep you from fulfilling
your desire to live a life that matters?

Women are particularly sensitive to relationships. You may need to revise your entire concept of relationships. A good way to do this is by recognizing relationship drainers.

Relationship Drainers

Relationship drainers are people who keep you from your goal of living to please God. These relationships cause you to be out of balance and influence you to lose focus on what is important. Here are some examples of relationship drainers:

1. Conflict creators. Some people are so unhappy with themselves that they pour out their anger on everyone else. Their relationships are filled with anger and strife that take a toll on others. Identify whether you are in a relationship with a conflict creator, and learn how to relate to that person without giving him or her the power to destroy your life or derail your focus.

When the conflict creator you identify is someone very close to you, such as your husband or mother, dealing with that person is more perplexing. You can only control what is in your power to control, yet you are still able to make decisions to bring balance to your life.

For a lot of women, being in relationship with conflict creators has a payoff. It might make them feel good about themselves. They can think of themselves as "better than" conflict creators because they keep their anger to themselves. Unfortunately, they fail to calculate the true price of this payoff.

Many women repress their negative feelings toward conflict creators. A lot of women are people pleasers, and conflict creators seek out people pleasers. You might have to stop and think hard before you realize that you are in a relationship with a conflict creator.

At the extreme, relationships with conflict creators can result in domestic abuse. In every abusive relationship there is a cycle of violence that includes a period of repentance by the abuser or conflict creator. This gives the woman hope that it will not happen again, but this false hope actually contributes to maintaining the violence.

THE CYCLE OF VIOLENCE[1]

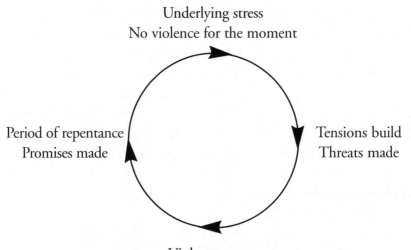

Underlying stress
No violence for the moment

Period of repentance
Promises made

Tensions build
Threats made

Violence erupts

Recognizing this cycle helps women comprehend that they are actually part of it. Often, a woman doesn't purposely provoke her partner, but she maintains the cycle by believing his promises that he will never be violent again. She takes him back into her arms and heart.

For this reason many states have adopted laws that allow a police officer who witnesses domestic violence to press charges against the husband or boyfriend. These laws were written after many years of frustration for officers when victims refused to press charges. The purpose of these laws is to help families begin the healing process.

If you are in an abusive relationship, I recommend that you recognize the cycle of violence and how you play an active part in it. Admit that you cannot make your spouse change. I urge you to talk to someone in your church or community who understands this cycle and can help you break free from it, and also get help for your husband or boyfriend.

Domestic abuse is an extreme example of how conflict creators can be a drain on your time, energy, and focus. The conflict creator in your life may not be as explosive. Perhaps your boss regularly takes out frustrations at work on you. Or your mom gets mad at you every other day because you didn't do things the way she wanted you to. It might be your ADHD son who throws fits in public or private. What can you do about your draining relationships with conflict creators?

If the conflict creator is your boss, you may be able to find a new job. There are times that the best response to a relationship that does more harm than good is simply to end it. In Philippians 1:15-18, Paul describes a group of conflict creators who were preaching the gospel out of envy and strife. They had selfish motives and hoped to stir up trouble for Paul, but Paul didn't pay them much attention. He didn't confront them or try to make them stop. In fact, he rejoiced because even if they were preaching out of selfish motives, at least they were preaching the gospel, and someone could be genuinely saved by their message. That was just fine with Paul.

There are some conflict creators we can ignore as Paul did. This doesn't mean we repress our hurt and anger, but instead we can acknowledge the hurtful behavior. We recognize that we can't change others, yet we can rejoice that we don't have to be bound by our bitterness and continual emotional upset.

When the conflict creator in your life is a child, husband, mother, sister, or other close relative, the same principles are at work, but they are applied differently. Our task with children is to discipline them and teach them how to have healthy relationships, establishing consequences for wrong behavior, and following through on what we say. We should not enter into the conflict or engage in a power struggle. I encourage parents to discipline in grief, not anger, to keep from escalating the conflict with the child.

When you say, "You will not watch TV tonight because you threw that ball at me," it comes across as a threatening, angry, powerful statement. The child is more likely to try to get more power for herself by responding, "Well, I don't want to watch TV anyway!" When you say, "I feel sad that I will have to take away your privilege of watching TV tonight because you threw that ball," it may not make your child any happier about the consequence, but it can defuse her anger.

There are some relationships with conflict creators that require us to confront misdirected anger. With a husband, a friend, or a mother, we may need to be like "iron that sharpens iron" (Proverbs 27:17), and be faithful in confronting the person about his or her anger. If, for example, your husband is regularly angry with the waiter or waitress who serves you, you may need to take a stand by not eating out with him until he learns to treat other people respectfully. Or it may be appropriate to tell your mother that if she continues to yell at you on the phone, you are going to hang up.

It is best in marriage and in friendship to cool down if a discussion provokes intense conflict. I'm not encouraging you to be a conflict avoider, because this is equally damaging to relationships. Still, it is often necessary to take a "time out" if your argument is getting heated and out of hand. Be willing to get back together to discuss the disagreement as long as the conflict between you will not involve intense anger, cursing, or other inappropriate expressions of anger.

2. Crisis junkies. You may also find yourself drained by people who are always in crisis and call you because "you are the only one who can help." While you may have a passion for helping others, if you don't learn how to respond to these people, they will deplete you and cause you to never want to help anyone again.

Emma eventually recognized that Jane was a crisis junkie. During their years of friendship, Emma always gave to Jane. That night, after a stressful day and evening, the last thing Emma needed was to listen to Jane complain about her life and how awful men are. But Emma felt compelled to listen and almost saw it as her duty. Taking care of Jane took a lot of time out of Emma's schedule and robbed her of quality time with her own family.

It's harder for women to set boundaries with crisis junkies than with conflict creators because crisis junkies are so needy it seems unchristian not to help the friend in need.

There is a delicate balance to be maintained. When a friend calls and can't breathe because she is crying so hard after she discovers that her husband is having an affair, it is important to be there for her. She may call in the middle of the night overwhelmed with fear and torment. Anybody's crisis will cost you sleep, time, and energy, and responding to it may be just the thing you are called to do by God. If another friend calls after learning her mammogram is questionable, as a good friend you will want to drop everything and offer comfort and support. You can never be prepared for a crisis; that's what makes it a crisis. When your friend calls, you give, but you sense that giving is something God has called you to do.

Most crisis junkies' relationships begin with legitimate crises. The unhealthy thing about Emma and Jane's relationship was that all their interactions grew from an unbalanced relationship in which Emma was the all-wise, knowing one and Jane was always needing help. When Emma evaluated her friendship with Jane, she felt it was salvageable, but not without some major changes.

When Emma and Jane met, they were equals—both new to town, single, and in their first jobs. After Emma got married and started her family, Jane was clearly jealous. Emma felt guilty for having such a good life, when a husband and children were all that Jane wanted. As a result, she became overly responsive to Jane's needs.

Emma decided to make some changes that gave her a significant part of her life back. She was honest with Jane about her guilt over having marriage and children when Jane didn't. They had a revealing heart-to-heart talk in which both voiced hurts and concerns that affected their relationship. The dynamic of their relationship changed after this talk, and the give-and-take became mutual again. Emma had actually been stifling Jane's growth by not requiring anything of her.

In crisis junkie relationships there is usually a point at which the crisis junkie wears the other person out and moves on to the next person. A true crisis junkie is not interested in taking responsibility for his or her actions like Jane eventually did. If a crisis junkie senses you are setting boundaries or inviting her to grow, she quickly finds someone new who will bear her burdens.

As a Christian counselor, I find that many people I work with want much more than I can give. God has called me to impart His wisdom and direction into people's lives for the difficulties they are facing. But people often want more: They want me to fix their problems. Some get angry when I don't fix problems, but most learn how to rely on God and the wisdom He has given them to make changes in their lives. A professional counselor wouldn't last long without setting boundaries with people in crisis.

Just as a lifeguard takes precautions when saving a drowning victim, so must a true friend take precautions when helping someone so that she does not get pulled down into her friend's crisis.

3. Interrupters. These relationship drainers can be either strangers or good friends. Though we are all interrupted from time to time, we can learn to control interruptions so that they don't control our lives. Even Jesus was willing to be interrupted occasionally, because of His compassion for people. We need to learn how to recognize worthy interruptions, as opposed to interruptions that steal our precious time and focus. Using caller ID and answering machines are great ways to skip sales calls and other interruptions.

Interrupters are less intrusive than crisis junkies, but they can keep you from reaching your goals. Perhaps a coworker consistently stops by to chat about nothing important, but she keeps you from doing tasks you are under pressure to finish. Pray for wisdom about how best to deal with these situations while not getting trapped by them. Be confident in saying, "I have some work to do. I'm not free to talk much right now." When someone calls and asks if you have a minute, explain just how much time you have for the call and be definite when it's time to hang up.

It's not that all interruptions are bad or wrong, but you should become assertive enough to deal with interruptions that damage your life. The key is being tuned in to what the Holy Spirit is telling you about how to respond to each situation. We want to be available to help others, while setting healthy boundaries. Ask yourself, "Why is this interrupter in my life?" "Is she here because God wants me to share His love with her?" "Is this interruption part of God's plan for my day?" "Is this interruption part of Satan's plan?"

4. Empty relationships. Empty relationships are one-sided and retained out of a sense of duty. Some women are unwilling to let a relationship go, even when it doesn't do a lot for them. Sometimes you outgrow a friend. That doesn't mean that you can't be friendly, but if your relationship takes a lot of effort with little return, perhaps it's time to let it go.

JoAnn ended up spending another long weekend with Cindy out of a feeling of obligation. She forced herself to go to the antique shops Cindy loved, while Cindy stayed in the night JoAnn went to a movie. JoAnn was the one who had set up this annual weekend getaway, though she didn't really want to. It seemed she and Cindy had very little in common anymore. JoAnn needed the freedom to stop forcing a relationship that wasn't there.

Planning an annual trip, making all the calls to Cindy, and attending the weekend didn't take up more than 48 hours of JoAnn's year, so maybe it wasn't such a big deal for JoAnn to keep the relationship ritual alive. But it didn't occur to JoAnn that maybe Cindy was responding just like she was, that she really didn't need or enjoy the relationship anymore and that it was okay to let it go.

It is okay to outgrow a friend. You don't have to feel like a failure if there are some friends that cycle out of your life. You might have a friend that you don't see for years, but you pick up exactly where you left off when you get together. Other friendships are meaningful and purposeful during certain times in your life, but they dissolve for no particular reason. You aren't angry or bitter, there's no moral failure, but there is a need for change.

Making decisions about what you can control in unhealthy relationships is very important to taking your life back. Existing in draining relationships can consume your time, energy, and effort if you aren't conscious of what is going on.

Relationships are crucial to our well-being as women. Just as draining relationships can do a great deal of damage in our lives, healthy relationships can produce strength within us. In the next chapter we will discover how to create healthy relationships.

Journal Exercise

Who are the people you have met with, talked on the phone with, interacted with, or spent free time with in the last year?

1. Pray for each person by name and ask God to reveal His will for you about these relationships.
2. Circle the names of those you believe God has blessed you with.
3. Underline the names of people who would fit the category of conflict creators. What can you do to resolve conflict in these relationships?
4. Put a check by the names of people you would consider crisis junkies. How does God want you to respond to these people?
5. Draw a line over any names of people who are interrupters. What can you do to manage their interruptions?
6. Create a prayer list of the people with whom you are in relationship, and ask God to give you wisdom to respond to each person in a way that glorifies Him!

Goal for the Week

Perform an act of kindness this week.

Chapter Twelve

Creating Healthy Relationships

But just as you excel in everything—in faith, in speech, in knowledge, in complete earnestness and in your love for us—see that you also excel in this grace of giving.

2 CORINTHIANS 8:7

*I*f you've never lived through a tragedy, then you may not recognize the importance of healthy relationships to the degree that Mary does. Mary thought life was great until her husband, Randy, threw her a curve ball she never saw coming. Returning from a weekend visit with her mother, Mary and her two children found their house transfigured. Randy had taken all of his clothes and personal items along with the family computer, television, DVD player, couch, and a few chairs. Randy was nowhere to be found, and Mary's heart sank when she peered into his empty closet, confirming that he had left her.

What could Mary do at such a shocking moment? She stood there with her two bewildered children who were looking to her for understanding. If the kids hadn't been watching, she might have screamed, thrown things, or pounded the floor, but she didn't want to add to the kids' hurt and confusion. Instead, she explained that she didn't know what was going on and promised to try to call Daddy to find out.

Before she called Randy, she called Karen, a friend from church who is just the right person to call during a crisis. Mary explained that she didn't know what to do and expressed her great concern for the children's response to her own reactions. Karen dropped everything and came right over, bringing her children, who were happy to go to their friends' house to play. When Mary's children saw Karen's, it was as if all their troubles vanished, and the foursome went off to play.

Karen answered the kids' questions, dug out snacks, and in general managed the play date. While all this was happening, Mary had her first opportunity to fall apart emotionally, get it back together enough to try to locate Randy, talk things over with Karen, and come up with a game plan to deal with this family crisis in the best way for the children.

There is no way Mary could have handled that day without Karen's help. The children would have heard hurtful conversations and Mary couldn't have handled her emotions as well.

Like so many women who face unwanted divorce, Mary was forced by her circumstances to reconstruct her life. Very little of the life she had been living the weekend she went to visit her parents was the same after she returned. Karen was there for her every step of the way. Though Karen wasn't a counselor and had never helped anyone go through a divorce and such radical change, Karen didn't falter. Her friendship and support were fundamental in helping Mary rebuild her life.

Having a support network is essential to living a life that matters. Healthy relationships are invigorating and get us through both the terrific and tough times. Jesus demonstrated how important it is to have healthy support systems as He set out on the ministry to which God called Him, recorded in Luke 6. As Jesus followed God's plan for His life, He enlisted friends who would aid Him on His journey and who would be influenced by Him in transforming lives.

There was a particular order to Jesus' friendships, which has been noted by Henri Nouwen. When I heard it, this message on the subject impressed me deeply, and I have wanted to model these kinds of relationships in my life as well. Nouwen taught that our relationships require solitude, community, and ministry.[1]

Solitude allows for a relationship with God. Luke 6:12 describes how Jesus went out to a mountain to pray and spent the whole night in prayer. Jesus had lots of room in His life for solitude with God, because His relationship with God was His most important relationship. All of His other relationships stemmed from this one.

Community springs from the kinds of relationships we are considering in this chapter. Jesus built community when He called the twelve disciples. Luke 6:13-16 describes how in the morning, after His night of prayer and solitude with God, He appointed the Twelve. Then, and only then, Jesus first began His public ministry. Luke 6:17 describes how He came down from the mountain to a level place and ministered to the multitudes.

Henri Nouwen said our relationships need to reflect that same order. He confessed that too often, he pursued ministry first. When he had a great idea for a way to impact people, he wanted to get right to it because it would work so well, and he was sure to get lots of people to like him. Then he wouldn't feel alone or useless.

Too many of us minister to others in this same way. We serve them, try to know them, and build relationships with them, all out of our own need to be loved. When this is the case, our relationships always backfire on us. We get depleted and become disillusioned because they can't give us what we expected. That isn't how you build healthy relationships. And, as we have observed, ministry that we do for ourselves will not be rewarded in heaven.

You build healthy relationships the same way Jesus did—by having a healthy relationship with God first. God gives you wisdom and discernment about the people who will support and guide you as you serve Him. What does it mean to build a relationship with God?

THE CENTERING RELATIONSHIP

Now, I don't expect you to travel to the nearest mountain (quite a journey for me since I live in Texas) and pray all night. The kind of solitude that Jesus demonstrated in His relationship with God was solid and mature. Most of us would do a lot of praying on that mountain, but our praying might consist mainly of pleas for God to bring us home safely and spare us from being eaten by a bear.

That's not the kind of praying Jesus was doing on that mountain. Jesus was already surrendered to the Father's love and care, and His prayers weren't the prayers of a baby Christian. When I think about the times Jesus got away to pray, I imagine Jesus and God communing and enjoying one another's presence. They may have pondered the wonder of their love for mankind. Maybe they enjoyed the sight of the universe viewed from a tiny spot on earth. I wonder if they delighted in the wildlife they had created. Did they consider the way an ant collects food and makes a home?

However this time was spent, it was total delight for Jesus, for as often as He could, He slipped away to spend time with God.

As I mentioned before, I have been trying to spend time with God every day since I was 16. Though I have missed more days than I like to remember, in general my Scripture reading has been a daily practice. I have spent long periods of time with God when I have traveled alone or attended a quiet retreat. It is always a delight, but it is also a struggle.

It's not as natural for me to be in solitude with God as it was for Jesus. In fact, on my first silent retreat I wrote about my struggle to be still with God. At the retreat I spent hours in a red canoe exploring a little lake with God. Here is my journal entry, written after this experience.

Still Waters

A still lake became a metaphor for reaching stillness in my soul. As I launched out in my red canoe, I was surprised by the crystal still water and how easy it was to maneuver through it. I felt like I was walking on water, gliding freely, hindered by nothing.

Then something occurred to me: I couldn't have found such freedom had I not put myself in the canoe. God became that canoe. He and He alone enabled me to enter so still a place without disturbing it. I discovered I couldn't enter stillness without placing my entire being, my whole self into Him.

The place of stillness He brought me to was beautiful to the eye. It was quiet everywhere I looked, but there were places of deeper stillness that I could not see. In order to go deeper into stillness I had to be willing to enter the unknown. I had to have the courage of a discoverer to go beyond the safety of the familiar. I had to be willing to let God lead me around bends, to waterfalls of unfamiliar origin. Most of all, I had to trust. I had to leave behind what I knew and move toward what I believed could be. I had to have faith.

And so by God's grace, I journeyed to deeper stillness. I found delightful hidden reservoirs of cleansing, refreshing waters. I heard the sound of the water gently rippling into a deeper reservoir. That reservoir was far beyond the reach of this day's journey, but He showed me its presence. He let me see that stillness is unlimited. I can go there again and again, and just like the universe, not conquer its recesses.

Though I enjoyed my time of stillness at the water's edge, where the reservoir flowed, I decided to leave. As I left the stillness the wind picked up, the waters rippled, a chill formed. My heart had fully received the stillness, but I also carried sin. A battle ensued as I wrestled with God in the wind and the waves and cold. I didn't want to surrender fully the contents of my heart. I enjoyed stillness, I drank it up, but I didn't want to leave my sin behind. There was a moment of surrender when I recognized my fear. I didn't want to surrender to God because I feared it would bring bigger storms, more wind, freezing rain.

So I sent out a fleece. Ahead of me were geese crossing the entrance of a cove. I asked God if they were sent to warn me not to go that way. I prayed that they would cry out against me as our paths intersected. I went in that direction, and in spite of my fears, I surrendered my sin, promising to forsake it. The geese seemed jubilant with my presence; they quietly praised my journey into the cove.

The lily-pad covered cove included delightful scents, sounds, and sights, the deepest stillness the lake offered. More quiet now than ever, I was free to rest completely in His love. This place of stillness felt complete, there was a need for nothing more. I basked in the sights and sounds. I was refreshed with cool, cold drink. I rested my weary shoulders and drifted in stillness complete.

The journey home was timeless. It felt as if the shore had been right there all along. I disembarked from my canoe and replaced it by the tree. No one else could know where I had been or that I was gone at all. There are no pictures to show, no souvenirs to remember, only a soul complete.

That experience exemplifies the possibility and the struggle in experiencing solitude with God. Stillness is what my soul craves, but it is so difficult to enter into. My fear of the unknown, my sin, my unbelief all hold me back from journeying deeper into a relationship with God.

Creating healthy relationships with others begins with your relationship with God, because without first fully receiving His complete love, you will always be trying to get others to love you as the sole purpose of being with them.

Your relationship with God energizes you, but God also created you to need others. God saw that there was one thing wrong in the garden He created: "It is not good for the man to be alone" (Genesis 2:18). God created us for relationship with Himself, but also for relationship with others. It is difficult, if not impossible, to live a life that matters outside the context of healthy relationships.

Relationship energizers are people who fulfill you and help you keep focused on reaching your goals. These relationships help you stay focused on the right things. Consider these examples of healthy relationships and decide if you are missing these in your life.

Examples of Healthy Relationships

Some women have no idea what a healthy relationship looks like. Here is a list of characteristics of a healthy relationship:
- In a healthy relationship you are accepted unconditionally.
- In a healthy relationship you are energized, not drained.
- In a healthy relationship you share the same values, or respect each other's values.
- In a healthy relationship the commitment is mutual.
- In a healthy relationship you are proud of each other's successes.

Finding a Mentor

Do you have a mentor, someone who is older and wiser and who can show you the way? A mentor is often not a friend for the whole journey, but one who demonstrates help and guidance in a specific area.

Connie considers her neighbor Sarah to be her mentor, though she has never told her so. Sarah would probably laugh at such a title, because she considers herself a good neighbor and nothing more. Sarah had prayed for whoever would buy the house next door, asking God to send her someone she could help grow in Christ. She felt a desire to live near someone she could bless. Sarah's youngest had just entered high school and the two older ones were in college. She had more time than ever but didn't want to work and miss out on these last years with her youngest child at home.

Connie didn't realize what a great deal she was getting when she and her husband bought the house next to Sarah's. When Connie and her husband moved to town, they decided Connie shouldn't get a job, since they were hoping to start a family. The first few weeks, Connie was glad that she didn't have the added pressure of a job while she unpacked boxes and decorated her new home. She had thoroughly enjoyed the chocolate chip pie Sarah brought over when she welcomed them to the neighborhood. After the first month though, loneliness set in, and she accepted Sarah's invitation for coffee.

Walking into Sarah's house was like walking into springtime. Sarah didn't have expensive furniture, but her home did have a clean, comfortable, loving atmosphere that couldn't be purchased from a design firm. Over time Connie began confiding in Sarah, at first simply asking for recipes and decorating and cleaning tips. Gradually their conversations developed into a deep friendship, one where Connie expressed her fears of infertility and doubts about her faith.

Informally, Sarah mentored Connie in how to have a relationship with God, how to manage a home, and how to be a good wife. Soon Connie got pregnant, and Sarah was available with helpful advice about the baby, as well as being an eager baby-sitter.

Perhaps you have a mentor in your life, though you never actually thought of her in those terms until now. Do you look up to someone who helps you grow as a person? Maybe it's a teacher from your Bible study or quilting class. I hope you have a mentoring relationship in your lifetime. When someone shows you the way because they have lived the way, they provide you with courage and encouragement to move forward.

Some women's groups set up mentoring relationships as part of their ministry programs, pairing an older woman who wants to be a mentor with a younger woman. They meet together informally, either for lunch or at each other's homes for prayer, and use the relationship to work on whatever is most needed.

Finding Someone to Mentor

Is there anyone who looks to you as a mentor? Do you demonstrate how to live in a certain area of your life? Being a mentor has many benefits to you as well as the other person—and not just spiritually, either. If you teach someone how to quilt, you probably enhance your quilting skills at the same time. It is energizing to have someone look to you for expertise and guidance about any subject.

We are all put on this planet to help one another, and we each have different gifts. I hope that as you consider your relationships, you can think of people you mentor. If you can't think of anyone, ask yourself why. Do you see yourself as too needy to help anyone else? Do you think you have nothing to offer others? I hope you will discover the joy of becoming an example or teacher for others.

Building a Support Network

In addition to benefiting from mentoring relationships, we all need to be energized by a special group of women we can depend on for support. In the day hospital and in out-patient treatment where I work, we offer support groups consisting of individuals dealing with similar emotional and mental health issues. These groups are very effective in helping people heal from problems, and I often recommend a support group as part of therapy.

When I write about building a support network, however, I don't mean a formal therapy group, but a group of individuals who help you get through difficult times. It's different from mentoring relationships in that your support network consists of mutually supportive friends. When you evaluate your relationships, can you name a few people you could call in the middle of the night if you needed to? Are you there for a few others in the same way?

To be adequately energized in life we need support from the relationships in our lives—friends to take us to the airport or look after the dog, pick up medicine when we are sick, or listen when we have important news.

Fun-Loving Spirits

In addition to other relationships, we are also energized by people who are just plain fun. Do you have some fun-loving spirits in your life? Are there people in your support network you can call to see a movie or share a cup of tea?

When I imagine Jesus' time with His disciples, I can't see them talking seriously 24 hours a day; there had to be joking and laughter too. I imagine Peter pulled a few practical jokes on the other disciples that made everyone laugh, and good-natured teasing went on throughout the day.

God has given us a sense of humor. He has given us a need to unwind and relax in a healthy way. Often He gives us relationships in which we can enjoy a good laugh. Life doesn't have to be serious 24/7. Your life is energized by fun-filled times when the conversation centers on laughter and love.

The Hungry

There is no doubt that Jesus wants us to take care of the poor. During the last week of His life on earth, He mentioned them several times: when Mary anointed His head with costly perfume (John 12:3); when He mentioned the sign of the saved (Matthew 25:35-36); when He urged us to love one another (Luke 4:18).

Do you ever wonder why you weren't born in a country impoverished by disease and war? Do you ever consider whether you would know God's love if you didn't live in a country where churches are built in every city and town? The poor will always be with us, and God is not deaf to their hunger pains, but all too often we are. There will always be those who have goods or wealth to give and those who are in need. If we lived our lives listening to the voice of God, maybe that help for the poor would be more conspicuous. Do you do anything to help others? It can make a huge difference in your own life.

I am amazed how much energy you can receive as you reach out and give to others. When the giving is led by the Spirit and not by the flesh, it fills you with pleasure and purpose. It is important to have relationships in which you give without expecting anything in return.

When I realized that my ministry is often to those who can at least afford to buy a book, I felt God calling me to consider another category of ministry. Our family budget includes giving to the poor and hungry. I make sure to read the monthly magazines from the ministries I support, especially Compassion International and World Vision. Their articles on conditions and difficulties around the world keep me in touch with the realities God deals with in His kingdom work every day.

It is easy to live in America and not think about whether you will have enough food to survive that day. When I read about the work my support benefits, I feel several things. First, I feel grateful to live where I live and am more thankful for the food and shelter I take for granted. Second, I feel appreciation for the individuals who are doing God's work in these needy places. Third, I am overwhelmed by how much more is needed and how little I can do personally.

It's like the story of the small boy at the beach after a tide left thousands of starfish stranded on the sand. The boy walked down the beach throwing the starfish back into the ocean, but there were thousands upon thousands still left. An older man said to the boy, "Why are you bothering with the starfish? There is no way you can make a difference." To which the boy replied, "I made a difference to that one," as he threw a starfish back into the ocean. The older man put down his things, walked out to the beach, and started throwing back one starfish at a time.

Each of us can do only what we can do. What would this world look like, and what would the state of the poor be, if each of us was faithful to do what we could? I wonder. Do you?

Relationships can be incredibly energizing on our journey here on earth. Make sure that you find the journey-mates God sends your way.

Journal Exercise

Relationship Survey
1. How does your relationship with God energize you?
2. Who are your supportive friends? List the names of people who fit in the following categories:
   - Mentor (one who mentors you)
   - Mentoree (one you mentor)
   - Support network
   - Fun-loving spirits
3. What do you need to do to build supportive relationships?
4. What relationships do you have that minister to others?
5. Review the checklist for healthy relationships on page 142. Consider issues you need to address with people in your life and make plans to address them.

Goal for the Week

Write a note of encouragement to each of the people who build you up and energize you.

Part Four

Keep Going! Maintaining Your Meaningful Life

Chapter Thirteen

Pillars of Time Well Spent

See, the Sovereign LORD comes with power,
and his arm rules for him. See, his reward is with him,
and his recompense accompanies him.
ISAIAH 40:10

*G*eorgene woke up feeling remarkably free. Her husband had left the afternoon before with both boys for a father-son campout. It had been an effort to get everything packed because Georgene's husband wasn't an organizer, so the burden had fallen on her. She had done it, with a little resentment that her husband wasn't more self-reliant. When she thought of them now, she knew that they were all settled in and, according to the weather report, should be having great weather all weekend. This was the first Saturday in ages that Georgene could remember sleeping until she woke up without an alarm clock. It felt good, really good.

For a while Georgene lay in bed enjoying the feeling of having no responsibilities. It felt like five or 10 minutes, but when she looked at the clock, she was surprised to discover she'd been lying there an hour. She got up and enjoyed a quiet breakfast attended only by her dog, who sat longingly at her feet waiting for a crumb to drop.

Lonely, she flipped the TV on to fill the quiet and found herself caught up in a movie filled with adultery and scandal, somehow unable to stop watching until it ended. As she was about to turn the TV off, she realized the next movie was one she had wanted to see, but had never had a chance to. And so she sat for three and a half hours watching TV in her robe.

Suddenly, it was lunchtime. Earlier in the week she had hoped to plan lunch with a girlfriend, but she never made any calls. Now, already 2:30 P.M., it was too late. She decided to treat herself by going out anyway, a good reason to take a shower and get dressed.

Georgene ate lunch at 4:00 P.M. by herself, wondering, *What is so great about having the boys gone for the weekend?* By the time she finished lunch, she felt like a total misfit with nowhere to go, and no one to spend time with. Depressed, she retreated to her home and once again turned on the TV to drown out her bad feelings. TV was boring, so she pulled out a novel she had already read and let it consume her mind until she ordered a pizza at 9:00 P.M.

Eating greasy food late at night gave her a stomachache, so now she felt lonely, rejected, and queasy. In addition, she felt guilty because her big plan for the weekend was to paint the guest bathroom, but she hadn't even gone to the store for supplies. She roamed around her house trying to forget how miserable she was until she finally got to sleep around 1:30 in the morning.

Georgene forgot to set the alarm for church the next morning and didn't wake up until it was too late to make the second service. As she lay in her bed looking around the room, she felt utter despair about how she had wasted the weekend. She did know she needed the extra sleep, but that was the only positive thing she had done. She spent the whole weekend without really spending it. It was gone, never to return, and she felt awful.

Have you ever had a weekend like that? One weekend is one thing, but when it becomes one weekend after another after another, the wasted time results in a habit of not really living.

King Solomon had some interesting observations about how to spend the time we have. Ecclesiastes 3:9-14 says, "What does the worker gain from his toil? I have seen the burden God has laid on men. He has made everything beautiful in its time. He has also set eternity in the hearts of men; yet they cannot fathom what God has done from beginning to end. I know that there is nothing better for men than to be happy and do good while they live. That everyone may eat and drink, and find satisfaction in all his toil—this is the gift of God. I know that everything God does will endure forever; nothing can be added to it and nothing taken from it. God does it so that men will revere him."

We think we would love a life that gives us freedom from responsibility and the luxury of leisure. But would we? Is there something about the toil of this life that teaches us to rely more heavily on God, thus giving us rich experiences? Do you discover the meaning and purpose of toil when you begin to fathom that this life is lived for eternity? How does living for eternity change the perspective of your life? According to Solomon, the pillars of a life well lived rest on these foundations: Be happy and do good.

Be Happy

Are there a few people that you would like to give this advice to? Maybe the grouchy types who can find something wrong with anything and everything?

Generally, being happy doesn't seem like the right goal for a Christian; after all, Jesus did promise us suffering. The happiness spoken of here, however, doesn't imply an absence of suffering or toil. In fact, the advice is to eat, drink, and find satisfaction in your toil. I would even go so far as to say, "If you aren't finding satisfaction in your toil, you are missing out on happiness."

Toil is not the result of sin. In Genesis 2:15 we read, "The LORD God took the man and put him in the Garden of Eden to work it and take care of it." That was before he had sinned. Sin did have an impact on the toil Adam (and all children of Adam) had to face. In Genesis 3:17-19 God warns Adam about the pain our toil would create as the result of sin. The ground would now be cursed and produce thorns and thistles that would make us work harder for our food.

Let's go back to Georgene and see what she learned about her wasted time. Eventually she got out her Bible to spend some time connecting with God, since she had missed church. She began by praying about her lost weekend and confessing her total inability to do the right thing. She asked God to show her what was wrong with her and help her to fix it. As she was reading Galatians 4, she heard God's answer in verses 6-7: "Because you are sons, God sent the Spirit of his Son into our hearts, the Spirit who calls out, 'Abba, Father.' So you are no longer a slave, but a son; and since you are a son, God has made you also an heir."

Georgene heard several messages in these verses. First, it was okay that she missed church that morning; she had done the right thing coming to Him rather than hiding from Him in her shame. Second, she heard that she was His daughter. She was not His slave, but a full heir with Jesus. She began to think about how much she felt like a slave to her husband and the boys. Yet this weekend her whole world seemed to fall apart without their presence. She knew she needed weekends like this, a break from responsibilities, but she also discovered how much it helped her to care for her family. And she learned that when she gets a little time for herself, she needs to use it to the fullest.

After her devotions, Georgene had a bite to eat and started getting the house ready for her three guys' return. By the time they got home, she was thankful for the laundry, the organizing she needed to do, and the task of putting away the camping equipment, sleeping bags, and fishing poles.

Funny thing, the resentment wasn't there the way it had been while she was packing for the campout. She found happiness in their need for her and her ability to provide what they lacked. She mandated showers for both boys, something their dad had not required, and insisted that they be checked for ticks and other residues of outdoor life. She looked back on the wasted weekend as a lesson in real happiness. It is not found in having nothing to do, but in the mind-set in which you do whatever you do.

Do Good

Now, here's a pillar of a life well lived that you can understand: Doing good for others. Who can argue with that? According to God's Word, doing good goes beyond the moment, with results that last forever.

This forever thing is difficult to get down; my son is the worst at it. He makes up his mind that he wants an $80 skateboard and asks for jobs to earn money to buy one. After he earns his first $5, he changes his mind about the skateboard and wants to buy an action figure for $4.99 instead. It seems impossible for him to wait for some future date when the reward for his hard-earned money will far exceed the $5 item. I'm no different. If I seek my rewards immediately, they will amount to nothing more, resulting in no future investment.

Doing good is like humility. It's hard to measure in yourself. If you really do good, you must do so from a pure heart, not one that is seeking reward. At the same time, it feels great to do good. That good feeling is self-satisfying. There's nothing wrong with that.

This raises the question, "How do you define good?" Doing good is not always understood by the world. Acts of kindness may go unnoticed on earth, but they make your soul happy, and they delight your Father. What is the will of God concerning you? Where are you doing good? Where are you obeying your Father? Where are you disobeying? How can you move toward the good life? God the Father will lead you to discover those "good things" that will help you invest in His kingdom. Be sensitive to His leading.

John was shocked by the impact of steel pounding into his rear bumper, and he quickly got out to look at the damage caused by the driver behind him. The driver jumped out of his car, cursing and screaming at John for stopping too quickly. John tried to keep his cool, while the irrational man carried on his tirade. John called the police to report the incident, and while the two waited, the other driver seemed to cool down a bit.

John recognized this man who had just smashed into his bumper as a neighbor who walked by his house regularly. Despite bitter conditions, John tried to defuse the other man's anger by being friendly. He mentioned that he thought he had seen him walking by his house every morning. John told him where he lived. The man settled down a bit when he realized they were neighbors and made the comment, "Aren't you the guy I see out every morning putting people's newspapers up on their porches?"

John was startled that this man would know that about him but admitted, "Yes, I am."

By the time the police arrived, the other driver had settled down and was willing to accept his responsibility for the wreck. He even apologized to John before the two went their separate ways. John's good acts may not be rewarded every day, and that is not why he does them, but they made a difference in this man's life.

In chapter four I mentioned my need to limit the amount of time I spent watching TV. I wondered what I could accomplish if I spent even half that time doing good instead of watching TV. How much happier would I feel? George Washington said, "Happiness and moral duty are inseparably connected." Galatians 6:9 tells us, "Let us not become weary in doing good, for at the proper time we will reap a harvest if we do not give up."

This book is not written to incite more guilt in already overburdened women. My purpose is not to condemn you and the way you live. Please don't feel that you have to fill every waking moment of every day wondering what you could be doing to impact eternity. You may be in a season of waiting before God. Don't be deceived about doing good, but remember that doing good is something God has called you to do.

Everything Is Beautiful in Its Time

God promises that if we are following Him, He will make everything beautiful in its time. A key to living a life that counts is learning to calculate the time factor.

For instance, when a parent loses a child to cancer, it is not a beautiful experience. Though time passes, life will never seem as beautiful after such pain and trauma. But there will be a time when that experience is made beautiful. In the meantime, there are glimpses of beauty in spite of the sorrow—beauty that comes from the promise of God's presence (Psalm 34:18). Beauty in the death of a child will never be fully seen on earth, but that doesn't mean we cannot experience the beauty of God's love and relationship while we struggle and seek to trust God in spite of the dreadful circumstances.

The apostle Paul assures us that our present sufferings are not worthy to be compared to the glory that will be revealed in us (Romans 8:18). If we really understood time, we would not get so angry with God about the suffering we endure on earth.

Jim Denison writes, "Time is the currency of the day. You may have more money next week than you have today—you will never have more time than you do right now. This morning you're one day closer to eternity than you've ever been. One day there will be no more time. Then what we did with our time on earth will have eternal consequence."[1]

Do you trust God to make all things beautiful in its time? The key to trusting God to make all things beautiful in its time is faith. Madeleine L'Engle writes, "We simply do not understand time. We know that a moving mass is necessary for the existence of time as we define it, and that time had a beginning, and will have an end. But try to define it, and you must reach the conclusion that time is a bit of a mystery."[2]

Because it is a mystery, we often undervalue time's significance in our lives. As Georgene's choices illustrate, it is too easy to waste time. The difference between Georgene and so many others is that she at least recognized how she was wasting the time she so valued. Most of us go from day to day, from project to project, from meal to meal, not really thinking about the value of time.

The time you are spending reading this book can be of immense value, if it is time during which you allow God to speak to you. Others may not think you are being very productive, sitting there reading a book when there are so many things to do. Perhaps you have let the laundry pile up or missed a meeting somewhere while you have used these minutes, this hour, to sit and read. Have you spent this time well? Has it been a valuable use of time?

As you reflect on time, you must accept the reality that you will simply be unable to be actively involved in something meaningful every moment of your waking life—not even every day for that matter. Just as we have seasons in the year filled with growth and activities, in other seasons growth is dormant. The seasons of our lives follow a specific cycle throughout the year, just like summer, fall, winter, and spring.

There are seasons of planting, nurturing, watering, and harvesting. There is also a season of waiting, which can be one of the most productive seasons of our lives.

As a newly married working woman I was busy working 50 hours a week and going to school 15 hours. I was busier than ever in my life but not very productive. I hadn't even quit work when I went into labor three weeks early. But the following years of staying home with my baby ignited creative energies that I never knew I possessed. I began leading women's Bible studies and was able to provide service and leadership in my church.

As my children have grown, I can see my life cycling through different seasons. There was a season in my life when God asked me to wait. He inspired me to write books and speak to women, but then told me to do nothing. My time of waiting was first of all obedience to God but also a time of great productivity, as God rid me of my selfish ambitions and wrong motivations. This was a season of tremendous spiritual growth and lessons in letting go.

Remember, we are not always in the season of harvest. We will regularly experience dormant times when it seems like nothing is happening with our lives from the outside. This does not mean that there will be no harvest. We need to be sensitive to the season for planting and follow the direction God leads.

Robert Morris explains it well: "We don't get there by pious aspirations, slavish copying of rules, well-polished public selves, or carefully guarded inner lives. We get there by the messier, slower path of learning step by step and mistake by mistake how to love, cooperate, forgive, trust, work through harsh and dark emotions. Part of the process of salvation, real soul healing and transformation, is in wrestling prayerfully with the rough places in our souls that resist Jesus' saving invitations. . . . Over time 'fruit' is born—a metaphor surely indicating the slowness of the process."[3]

We live our lives based on watches and calendars that tell us when to do what. Do we really think about the value of the time they are measuring? Too often we go through time without really thinking about it. That's what Emily discovered in the play *Our Town*. Emily died in childbirth and asked permission to return home to live just one day over again. After being gifted with this experience she asks, "Do any human beings ever realize life while they live it?" The stage manager answers, "No. The saints and poets, maybe. They do some."

Your time on earth is a gift God has given you. It is the gift that equalizes us in some ways and shortchanges us in others. This priceless gift is usually taken for granted, until we're late for a meeting or suddenly notice wrinkles that remind us we're getting older.

Time is most pressing to me when I am on my way home from a speaking engagement. As I leave on a trip, I don't mind spending time waiting in planes, airports, or hotel rooms. When the speaking is over and it's time to journey home, each moment I am away feels like eternity. A five-minute delay feels like five days. I have such a longing to return to my family that time seems to go on forever. I love this description of time by Henri Nouwen:

> Even though I often give in to the many fears and warnings of my
> world, I still believe deeply that our few years on this earth are part
> of a much larger event that stretches out far beyond the boundaries
> of our birth and death. I think of it as a mission into time, a mis-
> sion that is very exhilarating and even exciting, mostly because the
> One who sent me on the mission is waiting for me to come home
> and tell the story of what I have learned.[4]

What will you have to tell your Savior about your mission into time?

Journal Exercise

1. "If I could save time in a bottle . . ." What would you say was the best experience of time in your life? How much time did it involve? Was it a once-in-a-lifetime experience or can it be repeated? If it can be repeated, have you had this experience again? Why or why not?

2. Make a list of 10 ways to spend time that bring you personal happiness.

3. Make plans to do at least one of the things on your list this week.
4. Make a list of 10 ways you can do good for your family, friends, community, and world. Record how often you have done any on your list in the last year.

Goal for the Week

Don't watch TV for a whole week and consider how much more time you have.

Chapter Fourteen

Creating Accountability

So do not throw away our confidence;
it will be richly rewarded. You need to persevere
so that when you have done the will of God,
you will receive what he has promised.
HEBREWS 10:35-36

*L*ou had reached bottom. She decided she was done with compulsive overeating, so she spent six hours one afternoon researching an eating plan to follow and setting goals to make major changes in her life. She knew the way she was eating was wasting money and time, and keeping her from fully relying on God. The pleasure she received from food had become her anesthesia for dealing with stress, disappointment, unhappiness, and any other unpleasantness in life. She knew it, and God knew it, and she didn't like it. Everything was going to be different. Tomorrow she would change.

The next day Lou failed. She didn't fail because her plan was too strict. She had done her research and made healthy and workable goals to change her eating habits. She didn't fail because she hadn't hit bottom. In fact, she has felt like she had been at the bottom for decades and couldn't remember feeling free of shame, fear, and desperation to change.

So why did she fail? Lou failed because she didn't have a friend to share her journey. She was all alone and without accountability and support.

Maybe you know how Lou feels. Perhaps you have tried to change something in your life, such as your weight, your tendency to procrastinate, or your lack of organization, and found little success. You may have done your research too and discovered a foolproof action plan that went right down the drain after about two days.

One of the most important factors in successful self-improvement is accountability. But being accountable to yourself is like giving yourself a shot: You know the medicine is something you need, but it is hard to stick that needle in your own arm. It is much easier to get a shot when someone else helps you.

Living a life that matters is about change. Maintaining the change is the hard part. If you have ever had a new haircut, you know what I mean. You bring a picture to your hair stylist and ask if your hair can be styled that same way. She looks at the picture and gives you ideas, then does a beautiful job with your hair. You leave looking like a whole new you. But the next day, when you wash it, it's the same old style, only a little shorter. I've given up trying to maintain my haircut; it just doesn't look as cute when I do it myself. But I'm not giving up on living a life that matters. I won't get there without some accountability to myself, to God, and to a support network.

Accountability to Yourself

Your life is all you have to offer God as your thanks and appreciation for what He has given you. He won't make you serve Him. He won't make you live your life for Him. He has created you with a free will because He wants loving, obedient children. God wants your heart, and He has high standards. He won't accept the changes you are trying to make if you are changing to please your pastor, your husband, your mother, or your best friend. You need to freely and completely give yourself to Him out of love.

Paul was hammering that point home with the church at Corinth in 1 Corinthians 13. He said it like it is: "If I speak in the tongues of men and of angels, but have not love . . . I am nothing."

Ask yourself, "Why am I seeking meaningful changes in my life?" Is it because your Bible study leader did, and she is a good person so you want to do what she does? Or is it because you sense the full measure of God's love for you, and you want to order your life in a way that pleases Him?

Make absolutely sure that your journey toward living a life that matters is a response to God's love and you desire to obey His plan for your life.

I can guarantee that to live a balanced life, you will need to make changes and learn how to hold yourself accountable for them. Regularly ask yourself these questions:

1. Does your life reflect the priorities you set for yourself in chapter six?
2. Are you using your time and your energy in the areas that reflect your priorities?
3. What areas of your life are keeping you from working on your priorities?
4. Have you acknowledged your successes in making important life changes?

You will have an opportunity to respond to these questions in the journal exercise at the end of the chapter. It is best to set a time to check up on yourself. It is beneficial to check your goals and try to reread your journal at least once a month to review what God has been telling you.

Remember, Romans 14:10-12 reminds us not to judge our brothers, but to think about our own lives. "You, then, why do you judge your brother? Or why do you look down on your brother? For we will all stand before God's judgment seat. It is written: 'As surely as I live,' says the Lord, 'every knee will bow before me; every tongue will confess to God.' So then, each of us will give an account of himself to God." I encourage you to practice this accounting before God now, while you have the opportunity to change.

I love it when my children's schools send out mid-semester grades. It gives the kids a boost to know they are doing well, or it helps them recognize where they are weak while they still have time to change things. Give yourself a mid-semester grade. Think about where you are and where you are going. What grade would you give yourself?

Accountability to God

God is the source of your strength and genuine change. God is also your best cheerleader and encourager on the journey. Therefore, it's crucial to be accountable to Him.

The first time I went on a silent retreat, I expected God to use the time to point out my many failures. I was sure I needed a thorough evaluation of my deficiencies, and motivation to do better, sin less, and get myself in order. That is not at all what I experienced.

The last day of the retreat, I was reading my favorite chapter in the Bible, Romans 8. It starts out boldly, "There is now no condemnation for those who are in Christ Jesus." I sat there and cried as I experienced the feeling of no condemnation, a feeling that was foreign to me. The whole weekend I had heard and experienced God's delight in being with me. There were no lectures, no lists of my many shortcomings. Instead, I experienced complete acceptance.

God doesn't want to condemn me; I'm condemned already. God comes to save me (John 3:17-18). God is the most amazing accountability partner you could ever have. He gives you the strength (Philippians 4:13), and He gives you mercies that are new every morning (Lamentations 3:22-23).

When I think of the day that I will be asked to give an account of my life before God (Romans 14:12), I don't compare it to giving an account of myself before my third-grade teacher. Her name was Mrs. Jordan, and though everyone else called me Debi, she insisted that I be called Deborah. My mother confessed that Mrs. Jordan even scared her a bit. If I didn't get the lesson Mrs. Jordan was teaching, I felt like a total idiot. She rarely approved of anything I did, no matter how hard I tried, and she was unable to appreciate my unique efforts to learn.

In contrast, I think of my son's teachers. They seem to understand both his strengths and weaknesses in learning. When I bring my life before God, I don't expect to face condemnation about the ways I failed Him, but I will encounter His pleasure in the ways I lived well.

I find more victory over the sins in my life when I connect to God. I like to think of how to please Him, rather than how I can avoid His wrath. According to His Word, I don't have to worry about His wrath, not because of anything I've done, but because of what Jesus did for me (Romans 5:9-10). My only focus on being accountable to God is to please Him, not to avoid His judgment.

Accountability to a Support Network

Have you built a support network yet? Some of you may already be studying this book in a support network such as a Bible study. These types of groups are invaluable in women's lives. In fact, I think women grow, heal, and change in the context of supportive relationships. Perhaps an encouraging grandmother is part of your support network or your two best friends from high school. Whoever your group consists of, rely on these relationships to help you live in a meaningful way.

The need for support is one of the major issues I emphasize when people come to counseling for depression and anxiety. Isolation can cause depression. Remember, God said, "It is not good for the man to be alone" (Genesis 2:18). This is doubly true for women. Who do you count on for support?

Children love the Bible story about the four friends and Jesus (Luke 5:17-26). Jesus was teaching in an overcrowded home. Four friends heard that Jesus was nearby and thought of their friend who was crippled. They devised a plan to bring their crippled comrade to Jesus. Because he was unable to walk, he had to be carried on a mat.

We don't know how far they carried him, but we can imagine that his motionless body was heavy even when shared by four. I'm sure as they carried his cumbersome frame, they were counting off the steps to their destination. What a relief to their bodies and souls when they finally arrived at the home. But the room was so full of Pharisees and teachers of the law, there was no way for these four men and their paralyzed friend to get anywhere near Jesus. Rather than accept defeat, they decided to climb up on the roof and let their friend down through the tiles, right in front of Jesus.

After the letdown of coming so far only to be deterred by the crowd, they were probably fired up. Once they started up the roof, I'm sure there were snags to work out. Imagine how they managed to get their friend up on the roof and then to the ground through a hole. They hadn't planned on this before they left, so they probably had to improvise. They didn't complain; they just did it. They had come to this town to bring their crippled friend to Jesus, and nothing was going to stop them from completing their mission.

Think of how you might feel if you were one of those friends. They were probably huffing and puffing when they arrived at the home. Someone else might think, "Wow, I've done my best. I tried. Let's just go home." But these friends didn't seem to entertain such thoughts. They were determined to set their friend before Jesus, so they mustered up all the energy they had left and got their friend up to the roof. They removed the tiles and slowly lowered his heavy body, their muscles screaming for relief, sweat pouring off their faces.

Jesus noticed the faith of the four men just as much as the needs of the crippled man, and healed their friend's spirit and body. If you found yourself in that same helpless position, either physically or emotionally, whom could you depend on to carry you to Jesus? Do you have four friends that wouldn't give up on you and wouldn't give up their faith?

During a retreat, I was asked to consider this passage. The question was: "What if you were the paralytic in great need. Who would carry your mat?" We were told to name four people we could count on to carry us to Jesus—four people we considered strong enough in their faith to carry our bed if we were in great need.

I encourage you to answer the retreat leader's questions for yourself:
1. Who are four people that you could count on to help you in great need?
2. What does each of these people do for you?
3. What do you do for each of them?
4. Pray for each of them.

Accountability with Your Checkbook

Again, our checkbooks are another indicator of our journey toward living a life that matters. Real accountability is called for because checkbooks don't lie. You can review your progress in trusting God by evaluating how you trust God with your finances.

Accountability Calls for Celebration

Don't forget to celebrate your victories with God, yourself, and your support group. This makes accountability fun. Don't dread accountability, but look forward to it as an opportunity to confess your weakness and get back on track. Remember, a reward awaits you in heaven, and you can prepare by receiving a reward for a life lived well here on earth. Don't do all the work and miss out on the rewards of living a life that honors God.

Journal Exercise

Answer these questions:

Accountability to Yourself

1. Does my life reflect the priorities I set for myself in chapter six?
2. Am I using my time and energy in the areas that reflect my priorities?
3. What areas of my life are keeping me from working on my priorities?
4. How have I acknowledged my successes in living my life with meaning and purpose?

Accountability to God

1. What are you hearing God speak to you about this week?
2. Are you obedient to Him?
3. How has God encouraged or rewarded you this week?
4. What can you do to make sure you get closer to God and feel His pleasure about how you live your life?

Accountability to Your Support Network
1. Who are you accountable to about the changes you are making in your life?
2. When do you meet?
3. How has this person helped you as you make changes?
4. When was the last time you celebrated your successes?

Accountability with Your Checkbook
1. Does your checkbook reflect God's priorities for your life?
2. What actions can you make to change?
3. How would an angelic CPA evaluate your heavenly investments at present?
4. What goals do you have to give more of your resources to God's work?

Goal for the Week

Every time you open your checkbook, thank God for the resources He provides for you.

Living with Balance

*May the Lord make your love increase and overflow
for each other and for everyone else, just as ours does for
you. May he strengthen your hearts so that you will be
blameless and holy in the presence of our God and Father
when our Lord Jesus comes with all his holy ones.*

1 THESSALONIANS 3:12-13

*I*f I could summarize what I'm hoping you'll receive from reading this book it would be what Paul told the church in Rome:
"Therefore, I urge you, brothers, in view of God's mercy, to offer your
bodies as living sacrifices, holy and pleasing to God—this is your spiritual act of worship. Do not conform any longer to the pattern of this
world, but be transformed by the renewing of your mind. Then you will
be able to test and approve what God's will is—his good, pleasing and
perfect will" (Romans 12:1-2).

Isn't that what you want for your life? Don't you want to live your
years on this earth experiencing and doing His good, pleasing, and perfect will? I don't know many women who would answer no to that question. But you may be saying no in your heart without realizing it.

There are some final questions to ask yourself, now that you've
taken in all this information about how to live a life full of meaning and
purpose: "Do I really believe that God's will is good, pleasing, and perfect, or do I actually believe that my will is better?"

This is the crossroads. This is where you really change your life, or stay the same. This is your crisis of belief!

You see, you must believe Romans 11:33-36, "Oh, the depth of the riches of the wisdom and knowledge of God! How unsearchable his judgments, and his paths beyond tracing out! Who has known the mind of the Lord? Or who has been his counselor? Who has ever given to God, that God should repay him? For from him and through him and to him are all things. To him be the glory forever! Amen."

Can you say a hearty Amen to that? Do you believe God? Do you believe God is full of the riches of wisdom and knowledge? Do you believe that His judgments and paths are beyond tracing out? Do you understand your utter poverty before God? Do you hold to the certainty that all things are from Him and through Him and to Him? If you say yes to all those questions, if your heart cries out in belief, if you are assured of who He is, then you will want to respond.

The way you respond to God's goodness is to offer your life as a living sacrifice. Romans 12 provides a summary of how to make over your life. Romans 11 gives the motivation, the reason to live in a transformed manner. It is because God has woven into the fabric of the earth and His people some truths, a way of moving toward Him, a way of knowing Him and healing one another. The God who needs no counselor has given you instructions that are guaranteed to bring life.

Once you grasp the reality of God and His overwhelming mercy toward you, there is no other response than to offer your life. My favorite hymn is "When I Survey the Wondrous Cross," written by Isaac Watts. One line goes, "Were the whole realm of nature mine, that were a present far too small; love so amazing, so divine, demands my life, my whole, my all."

These words reveal an amazing irony. What would you want if you had everything? Would you want a universe, or would you want me to offer my life in service to you? As for me, I think I would take the universe. Isaac Watts speaks the truth of what God wants. He already created the universe. It was His. He gave it to us to rule, and Satan has attempted to take it over for himself. God didn't send His Son to claim back the universe. God sent His Son to get you back, to give you the opportunity to come back to Him, to make it a possibility that you would offer your life to Him. God doesn't want me to go out and make Him a universe; He wants me to believe Him, accept His power, and yield my will to live my life according to His plan.

Living your life with purpose according to God's Word and God's plan is your spiritual act of worship, the way you show God how fully you receive His mercy, love, and grace. Presenting your life as a sacrifice is your small gift to your wonderfully kind Benefactor. Sometimes you receive gifts that you enjoy and appreciate, prompting a desire to return the favor on the next occasion. Other times you receive a gift so valuable there is no way you could repay it. Maybe someone gives you the gift of a paid vacation or something else far beyond the scope of your wages. The giver doesn't expect you to return the gift equally, but he or she appreciates your grateful response. That is how God receives our little lives; they are the grateful thank-you notes we write.

We give our lives to Him by choosing not to conform to the pattern of the world. People grow up, go to school, learn to read and write, get a job, buy a home, have children, retire, and die. We do what is expected of us. We may even go to church if that fits in with what we think others want. It can mean abusing alcohol and drugs, indulging in unmarried sex, and making other wrong choices, but it can also include doing what is considered good by the world. Conforming to the pattern of the world isn't always something negative.

I distinctly remember being 13 years old and deciding that I wanted to see what the world had to offer. I looked at my older siblings and saw them doing what Mom and Dad would want, involved in youth group and following the rules. I said to myself, *Is that all there is? I think there might be a better way to live out there.* I set out to find it. It took me two years to discover there wasn't anything better out there and to come back to God, but it has taken me decades to get the influence of the world out of my mind. It is a daily struggle to be transformed from the pattern of the world by the renewing of my mind.

I've discovered a litmus test to help me determine if I am thinking according to the pattern of this world or according to a transformed mind. The test is whether I think that God's will is good, pleasing, and perfect.

When I am thinking according to the pattern of this world, I am not thinking highly about God's view of things. For example, I teach a sexual intimacy session to the newlywed classes at my church and boldly explain that sexual intimacy is meant for married couples. I ask the couples who are already having sex to make a commitment to each other to stop having sex until their wedding night, out of obedience to God. Many Christians believe it is okay to have sex if you are in love and planning to get married, but God's Word says sex is for married couples.

Some of the faces I look into as I am teaching the class reveal that they really don't think I have a clue about what is going on in the world. Some believe I am an out-of-touch minister's wife who doesn't understand the real world. I do understand the real world, but I still trust God and His Word any day over what the world says is okay. God has good reasons for telling us not to have sex before marriage. When I see God as loving and all-knowing, I will trust that His will is best, better than mine, outshining anything the world offers me.

In order to surrender my life to God, I need to stop thinking of myself more highly than I ought. Romans 12:3 goes on to instruct me to think of myself in sober judgment. When you are afraid to let God have control of your life, you are drunk on your own wisdom, and let me tell you, that is dangerous. God has given you a measure of faith. This faith will direct you to the way your specific life should be lived. Your life will not look just like my life, and your best friend's will be different from yours as well.

Romans 12:4-8 explains the unique combination of gifts God has given to us to be used by the church. This means that I have a purpose in the church that others do not have, and others have purposes that I don't have. You don't make meaningful changes in your life for yourself alone. You make them according to God's plan for the building up of the body of Christ. You don't make life changes so you can be happy with what you do now; you make over your life so others receive spiritual benefits from your obedience to God. How are others receiving spiritual benefits from knowing you?

When you live a life that matters, your life becomes a living sacrifice. That's the kind of life that gets rewarded, the kind of life that is pleasing to God and that gives you joy and hope.

Paul concludes this chapter with some final instructions that lead to a life that is perfect, pleasing, and delightful to God:

First, love sincerely (Romans 12:9). Don't try to copy goodness; you have to have the real thing. Don't try to love in your own strength; it won't be good enough. In order to love sincerely you must receive God's love fully. When your desire to love flows through Him, it becomes sincere. The only way to discover sincere love is to build your foundation on God's love.

Next, know what to hate (v. 9). You are told to hate what is evil and cling to what is good. You will need to do this with almost every person you meet. In fact, that would be a good experiment for you this week. Think about what is evil or negative in a person and hate that part of him or her, but cling to what is good about the person. Apply this to the television shows and movies you view.

When it comes to your relationships, be devoted to others and honor others above yourself (v. 10). What better picture of this can you find than how God relates to us? Can you imagine anyone more devoted to relationship than He is with us? Can you think of anyone who honors you more than God?

Keep your spirit connected to God's Spirit; don't give up! Verses 11-12 encourage us to never lack in zeal and be joyful in hope and patient in affliction. The key to displaying this kind of attitude is faithful prayer! Never underestimate the power of God's Spirit.

In regard to others who are in need, share! Verse 13 tells us to share with God's people who are in need and to practice hospitality. God is pleased when you share with your fellow Christians. Many times, it is the love shown by responding to a need that opens someone's heart to Christ.

To whom do you give blessings? Those who persecute you (v. 14). Why wouldn't you curse those who persecute you? Doesn't that make more sense? Verses 19-20 tell us to avoid seeking revenge against enemies, but to leave room for God's wrath. Feed your enemy if she is hungry; give her something to drink if that is what she needs. Why? Verse

21 holds the key: so you won't be overcome with evil but will be able to overcome evil with good.

With whom do you rejoice? Those who rejoice (v. 15). With whom do you mourn? Those who mourn. Enter into people's lives, and enter into people's pain. Don't categorize people. Don't be proud or conceited, or think they aren't your kind of people (v. 16). See everyone as God's child and live in harmony, without division regarding your beliefs, financial status, or skin color.

One last piece of advice on your relationships: "If it is possible, as far as it depends on you, live at peace with everyone" (v. 18). It is not always possible to have peace in your relationships. Jesus offers peace to everyone who will have a relationship with Him, but unfortunately, not everyone responds to His offer.

In my counseling office I meet people who are troubled by damaging relationships. Often these relationships are with individuals who died years ago. This scripture clearly says to look at your life and do the forgiving, loving, and offering—but having peace in your relationships is not solely dependent on you. One evidence of a purposeful life is that you are living with the knowledge that you have done as much as you can possibly do to create peace in your relationships.

Romans 12 offers us a good way to make sure you stay focused on living a life that matters, becoming a pleasing sacrifice to God. It is worshipping 24/7. It is grasping the idea that your life lived for God is awesomely pleasing to Him, but it is also the most satisfying life you could possibly live here on earth. You aren't living just for the here and now but for a present and a future centered on the amazing, perfect love of a Father who would give everything to adopt you as His child.

When you choose to live your life as a pleasing sacrifice to God out of worship, the positive changes you are making take on a whole new perspective and motivation. Miriam Pollard explains it this way:

> This is not your project. It is God's. It needs prayer and it needs the
> relaxed attitude of someone who leaves the results in God's hands,
> content with the privilege of trying. We are not forcing our virtue
> on God. He has no obligation to make it turn out as we wish. We

are giving ourselves to him in this particular form, not demanding of him that he make of us what we want. It is, as the older terminology put it, a supernatural proposition. We are not using God as an instrument in our self-improvement scheme. We are not forcing him into making of us something we will get a kick out of being![1]

Keeping your life in balance means you will need to come back to this reality over and over again as you live for God. Don't worry. If you are serious in your desire to live for God, He will remind you when you get off track, which you will inevitably do.

Miriam's words penetrate into the selfish motivations of my soul. Too often I want to live a life that counts because I will get a kick out of being that type of woman. She says I'm not to use God as an instrument in my self-improvement scheme; rather I am to lay my life down as a living sacrifice. I'm to be just as willing to feed the poor or change a dirty diaper in the church nursery as I am to write a Christian book or speak at a retreat. My aspirations are to fully give myself to God in His service, not to get more people to like me and think I am a godly woman.

Being Prepared

During the last week of Jesus' life here on earth, He taught His disciples about being prepared for His return. They asked Him to describe the signs of the coming of His kingdom. The disciples were eager learners, wanting to know everything they could to be ready for Christ's return.

Jesus told the disciples to lead watchful lives. He says the same to you and me. Don't just move from appointment to appointment, duty to duty, crisis to crisis. Keep your eyes open, and really see what is happening around you every day.

What should you be watching for? According to Matthew 24:42-47, be aware of God's work here on earth. Jesus the Master has gone away for a little while, but when He returns, He wants to find you faithful in managing the world. Are you taking care of the Master's people?

Are you sharing Christ with them? Do you have the mind-set of the Master? Do you set your heart on the things that delight Him?

According to Jesus, it's not so hard to wait for the Master to return. There is plenty to do every day. Just believe that He will return, and do those things you know will please Him when He does come back for you. Think about how you lived this past year. If Jesus were to return today, what are the things that you are glad you took part in last year? What are some of the things you wished you hadn't done at all? If you are waiting for His return, what are you doing this year to prepare for His arrival?

Micah 6:8 sums up a life that pleases God. "He has showed you, O man, what is good. And what does the LORD require of you? To act justly and to love mercy and to walk humbly with your God." Justice, mercy, and humility are three foundational attributes of a person who longs to serve God. Justice and mercy cannot be experienced without true humility. If you begin by understanding your humbly favored position before God, the outflow should be love of justice and mercy—a truly changed life.

Checking for Balance

How have you changed as a result of reading this book and listening to what God has said to you through these words? Let's consider the seven characteristics that have been the focus of this book.

1. You feel loved and accepted by God. Miriam Pollard makes a strikingly truthful statement: "But watch it—he is not nearly so interested in the perfect product as we are."[2] Our sin nature compels us to compare and evaluate our use to God against that of His other servants. We even want to judge ourselves against ourselves. We like results. We want to get there. We want to be finished with sin. We want to reach the place spiritually where we will no longer be plagued by anger toward other drivers, or jealous of other women, or envious of our neighbors.

We can become too goal-oriented in making life changes and miss the whole point. Our purpose is to please God, to make Jesus smile. We want to show our thankfulness and grasp our utter poverty before Him. When we serve God His way, we must let go of what we want ourselves to become, realizing truly what we have become. We are His workmanship created for good works in Christ (Ephesians 2:10). We are accepted, we are loved, we are His.

2. You trust God's wisdom for your life. Have you discovered the secret ingredient to serving in the kingdom of God? When you do what you do in and through Him, it just gets done in incredible ways.

Honestly, I don't have time to write this book, serve my church, serve my family, and keep up with the day-to-day issues of life. I don't know how I ever accomplished what I accomplished this very week. I am learning when I do it on my own, I fail, but there is true freedom and joy in ministry when I do it in Christ. This week alone I have spoken a couple of times, gone to both kids' sporting events, had two wonderful social occasions, worked, worshiped, and lived an abundant life. I even watched a favorite movie. If it is truly God's plan, you will have God's strength to do it (Matthew 11:28-30).

3. Your life—calendar, checkbook, experiences—reflects your priorities of relationship with God and loving others. The pioneer missionary to China, Hudson Taylor, carried many burdens because of his effort to reach the Chinese people with God's Word. There was a dramatic change in his spiritual life, and others noticed the way he began to handle his increasing burdens. A fellow missionary wrote, "He was a joyous man now, a bright, happy Christian. He had been a toiling, burdened one before, with latterly not much rest of soul. It was resting in Jesus now, and letting Him do the work—which makes all the difference!"[3] There was a time in Hudson Taylor's life that he released his burdens to God and never took them back.

When will you learn this secret? Have you yet?

4. You know how to deal with relationships that drain your energy, and you establish proper boundaries. How are you handling those relationships? Are you depleted by the lack of forgiveness in your life?

Forgiveness is a wonderful blessing God has given. I am so glad that He loves me enough to teach me how to forgive, as He has forgiven me. My soul has been transformed by the supernatural healing power of forgiveness.

Are your relationships balanced by friends who truly energize you and help you along your journey?

5. You take care of your physical energy needs. Your heart functions like a little timer that reveals how long you have left to live for Him. You cannot guarantee that by taking care of your body you will live a long life. You could be in great shape and die in a plane crash tomorrow. But it's necessary to manage your health if you long to serve God.

6. You live in financial freedom. Don't be discouraged if you aren't free from financial bondage yet, but do notice that this area of your life may have more of a negative force than you realize. Financial bondage can prevent or prolong readiness to do God's will. It can hold you back from receiving all that He desires for you. It is worth working on your finances to be prepared to live your life for God.

7. You sense God's pleasure with you. Above all, my purpose in writing this book is to draw you closer to ordering your life in such a way that you know, beyond a shadow of a doubt, it pleases God. I long for you to experience the exhilarating feeling of knowing His delight in you. This is what keeps me pursuing a life that matters, thinking about how to put a smile on the face of Jesus.

I love this excerpt from the Paschal Homily of St. John Chrysostom:

> If any have wrought from the first hour, let him today receive his just reward. If any have come at the third hour, let him with thankfulness keep the feast. If any have arrived at the sixth hour, let him have no misgivings; because he shall in nowise be deprived therefore. If any have delayed until the ninth hour, let him draw near, fearing nothing. And if any have tarried even until the eleventh hour, let him, also, be not alarmed at his tardiness. For the Lord,

who is jealous of his honor, will accept the last even as the first. He
giveth rest unto him who cometh at the eleventh hour, even as unto
him who hath wrought from the first hour.
And He showeth mercy upon the last, and careth for the first; And
to the one He giveth, and upon the other He bestoweth gifts. And
He both accepteth the deeds, and welcometh the intention, and
honoreth the acts and praises the offering.
Wherefore, enter ye all into the joy of your Lord; Receive your
reward, both the first and likewise the second.[4]

You see, pursuing a life that matters isn't about comparing yourself
to others. It's not an achievement. It is a gift. It is an understanding of
what life is really all about. It is a relationship with a God who is loving
and good. I pray this truth of His love and delight in you will mold your
life into a deeply fulfilling adventure with a loving God.

"For the Lord himself will come down from heaven, with a loud
command, with the voice of the archangel and with the trumpet call of
God, and the dead in Christ will rise first. After that, we who are still
alive and are left will be caught up together with them in the clouds to
meet the Lord in the air. And so we will be with the Lord forever. Therefore encourage each other with these words" (1 Thessalonians 4:16-18).
I look forward to meeting you there!

Journal Exercise

Answer again these questions first posed at the beginning of this book:
1. When you think of your relationship with God, do you feel
   guilty or wrong?
2. Are you afraid to yield your life to God's plan because He may
   have more for you to do than you are already doing?
3. When you look at your calendar, checkbook, and daily experiences, do they seem like heavy burdens to bear?
4. Do you have relationships that deplete you?
5. Do you ignore your bodily signals for rest, good nutrition, and
   exercise?

6. Are you in financial bondage?

7. Do you sense God's disappointment in the way you live your life?

I hope you are on your way to answering no to every one of these questions.

Goal for the Week

Every time you see the moon and stars, remember that God loves you more than the universe.

Appendix
Leading a Study

❃

One-on-One Discipleship Relationship

This book is an ideal guide for two or three women who want to meet together to grow in their relationship with God. If God has put someone on your mind to study this book with, I encourage you to pray for that person and give her a call to find out about her interest. It just may be that if you study this book together, you will gain a stronger spiritual friend, develop a closer relationship with God, and make over your life, all at the same time.

When you are studying this book with just one or two people, you have greater flexibility. The first time you meet, you could decide how often you want to meet and where you would like to discuss what is going on in your lives. Some women are comfortable talking like this in a public place such as a coffee house, while others prefer to be in a private home.

I recommend that you meet weekly or at least twice a month. If you only meet monthly, you might consider doing at least two chapters a month so you don't lose the consistency of what you learned in the previous chapter.

When you meet, you can share results of your Journal Exercises, as well as any insights, breakthroughs, or failures you experienced between meetings.

When you choose a study partner or group, be sure you have people who are comfortable sharing about failures as well as victories. You need someone who can encourage, but not judge. Look for someone who:

- accepts you unconditionally,
- doesn't drain your energy,

- shares your values,
- offers mutual support, and
- is proud of your accomplishments.

Refer to chapter twelve for details. I hope you will find someone who knows that true change comes from relying solely on the Holy Spirit.

An outline of your meeting may flow like this:

1. Greetings
2. Prayer
3. Journal Exercises
4. What did you learn from your goal for the week?
5. Ask each other: What do you need most from our meeting tonight?
6. Exchange prayer requests with each other
7. Celebrate victories

I'm trying to stay away from mandating how your informal time will flow while giving you ideas about how to use this time, if you haven't been in this type of accountability relationship before. I pray your time together with a friend will solidify the truths God has been teaching you and help you gain new insights and ideas about how to be aware of His love for you and His plan for your life.

Using This Book as a Bible Study

The content of this book will make a great Bible study. However, I didn't limit it to a Bible study because I wanted it to be used one on one as well. The following ideas may help you offer this as a group Bible study in your church or home.

Getting started. If you plan to lead a Bible study based on this book, read the text and answer the questions of at least the first two chapters before you begin the study. You may choose to read through the entire book ahead of time if you wish, if you haven't done so already. The other women will be looking to you for guidance, and it is helpful to have some familiarity with the book and its message before you begin the study.

Publicity. You will be in charge of publicizing your study and inviting women to join your group. You will also organize the place, time, and dates of meeting. You may be leading this study with a group that is already in existence, such as a book club, Sunday school class, or support group. In that case, the only publicity you will need is to announce the dates that you will begin the study and discuss how to purchase books.

If you are publicizing this study in your church, you should discuss the best ways to do this with your church staff. They will have an idea of how far in advance to begin publicity and how to handle sign-up. If you are meeting at the church, you will want to follow the procedures your church has for reserving a room for your meeting. If your group meets in a home, you need to make those arrangements and include meeting times, dates, and places in the publicity materials.

Organizing the study. There are 15 chapters in this book, which may be too many for your Bible study semester schedule. If you need to condense the weeks, I would suggest you combine several chapters. For instance, if you needed to fit it into a 10-week session:

Week One	Chapter One
Week Two	Chapters Two and Three
Week Three	Chapter Four
Week Four	Chapters Five and Six
Week Five	Chapter Seven
Week Six	Chapter Eight
Week Seven	Chapter Nine
Week Eight	Chapter Ten
Week Nine	Chapters Eleven and Twelve
Week Ten	Chapters Thirteen, Fourteen, and Fifteen

Lesson plan. If your Bible study meets for an hour, you could give an overview of the chapter(s) you studied that week. At the end of this section you will find an index of all Scripture mentioned in the chapters to help you organize your thoughts around God's Word.

The second half hour could be used for discussion. Most of the material the women will write about each week is personal, so they'll need to feel comfortable sharing their answers to the Journal Exercises in the small group. You know the group you are dealing with, so use your discernment to decide whether to have women share their responses to the Journal Exercises as a part of the discussion. It would be great if the women felt comfortable sharing about how God is speaking to them.

As an alternative, you could list four to six discussion questions based on the material you present in the first half of the lesson. These questions should be general in nature and not require individuals to share personal information. For example, questions for chapter one might flow like this:

1. Why does the Bible say it is important to be careful how we live? (Ephesians 5:15-16)
2. How was the apostle Paul's statement in Philippians 1:21 significant in his effort to live a life that counts?
3. Could you relate to Emma or Madge in the way they answered those seven bold questions?
4. What were the ancients (historical biblical characters) commended for in Hebrews 11?
5. Describe the kind of life you think makes God sad.
6. Describe the kind of life you think pleases God most.

Create an atmosphere for sharing. I find it helpful to create an atmosphere of sharing by setting some group rules:
- All sharing is voluntary.
- All comments shared will be kept confidential.
- We are here to love and support one another.

You could ask group members if they would like to add more rules and give their feedback.

As the leader, you might set the right atmosphere by sharing your personal reflections on making meaningful life changes, either after reading this book or through other experiences you have had. If you don't feel you've quite reached this goal, you might share where you are in your spiritual journey and what it is you hope to accomplish through this study.

Many leaders are afraid of silence. Give women time to share. Be sensitive to those who are reluctant to talk in groups by gently encouraging them to share, yet never forcing them. Don't let one woman dominate the whole discussion time. Try not to put anyone on the spot or make her feel foolish for the response she gives.

I encourage you to pray for each participant. Ask God to give you the wisdom to lead the group. Some discussion questions don't have right or wrong answers, but if someone is saying something that contradicts Scripture, it is your responsibility to gently but firmly state the truth from Scripture. This is a lot of responsibility, but remember that the Holy Spirit is there to give you the wisdom you need.

Prayer. There is a special intimacy that develops as women pray for each other. You can assign prayer partners or have a prayer list where women share prayer requests. Women love to talk, so be sensitive to the best way to facilitate prayer in your group. You may want to have a list so they can write their requests and make copies right after the study for women to take home for later prayer.

I want to personally thank you for the gift you are giving to God and the women you serve through your leadership.

Notes

Introduction

1. Dr. Deborah Newman, *A Woman's Search for Worth* (Wheaton, Ill.: Tyndale House, 2002).

Chapter Three

1. Generosity (Hillsboro, Kans.: Sound Principles, 1985).

Chapter Four

1. Newman, *A Woman's Search for Worth*, pp. 78-79.

Chapter Five

1. Henry Drummond, *The Changed Life* (Titusville, Fla.: Soul Care, Inc., 1988), p. 7.
2. Ibid., p. 8.
3. Ibid., pp. 10-11.
4. From a sermon titled "When the Bombs Fall" given by Dr. James C. Denison, Senior Pastor, Park Cities Baptist Church, Dallas, October 14, 2001.

Chapter Six

1. Henri Nouwen, *Life of the Beloved* (New York: Crossroad, 1992), p. 28.

Chapter Eight

1. Ronald Blue & Co., LLC. (www.ronblue.com/services_financial.html) and Crown Financial Ministries (www.crown.org).

Chapter Ten

1. Brother Lawrence, *The Practice of the Presence of God* (New York: Oneworld Publications, 1999).
2. Brother Lawrence, quoted in *Christian Classics in Modern English* (Wheaton, Ill.: Harold Shaw, 1991), p. 26.
3. Ibid., p. 33.
4. St. Augustine, quoted in *Christian Classics in Modern English* (Wheaton, Ill.: Harold Shaw, 1991), p. 240.
5. Miriam Pollard, *The Laughter of God* (Wilmington, Del.: Michael Glazier, 1986), p. 54.
6. Nouwen, *Life of the Beloved*, p. 85.
7. Joan Chittister, *Wisdom Distilled from the Daily* (San Francisco: HarperSanFrancisco, 1990), p. 99.

Chapter Eleven

1. Adapted from the original concept of Lenore Walker, *The Battered Woman* (New York: Harper and Row, 1979).

Chapter Twelve

1. From a sermon given by Henri Nouwen at First Presbyterian church, Ft. Worth, Texas, March, 1994.

Chapter Thirteen

1. Dr. James C. Denison, "What's Worth More Than Money?" *The Word Today*, Park Cities Baptist Church, Dallas, Mar. 7, 2002.
2. Madeleine L'Engle, *Walking on Water* (Wheaton, Ill.: Harold Shaw, 1980), pp. 94-95.
3. Robert C. Morris, "Enlightening Annoyances: Jesus' Teachings as a Spur to Spiritual Growth," *Weavings Journal*, Sept./Oct. 2001.
4. Nouwen, *Life of the Beloved*, p. 110.

Chapter Fifteen
1. Pollard, *The Laughter of God*, p. 74.
2. Ibid., p. 48.
3. V. Raymond Edman, *They Found the Secret* (Grand Rapids, Mich.: Zondervan, 1984), p. 1.
4. Paschal Homily taken from Pravoslavie.RU© (www.pasvoslavie.ru/english/paschalhomily.htm).

Scripture Index

❁

Chapter One

Psalm 39:5: "You have made my days a mere handbreath; the span of my years is as nothing before you. Each man's life is but a breath."
Eph. 5:15-16, Heb. 4:12, Phil. 1:21, Heb. 11

Chapter Two

Philippians 3:20: "But our citizenship is in heaven. And we eagerly await a Savior from there, the Lord Jesus Christ."

2 Cor. 5:10, 2 Tim. 4:7-8, Phil. 1:21, Rom. 12:1, Heb. 11:6, Matt. 6:33, Luke 16, Rev. 4:10-11, Gen. 15:1, 1 Cor. 9:25, Col. 3:23-24, 1 Thess. 2:19, 2 Tim. 4:8, 2 Peter 3:11-14, 2 Peter 3:9, Rev. 2:10, James 1:12, 1 Peter 5:4, Ezra 7:10

Chapter Three

Colossians 3:1-2: "Since, then, you have been raised with Christ, set your hearts on things above, where Christ is seated at the right hand of God. Set your minds on things above, not on earthly things."

2 Cor. 12:4-9, Rev. 22:12, Rom. 14:12, Rom. 2:6, 16, Prov. 24:12, Isa. 40:10, Psalm 62:12, Matt. 16:27, 2 Cor. 5:10, Rev. 20:11, 2 Cor. 8:7, Matt. 6:5-8, 6:16-18, 19-21. 1 Cor. 9:17, 1 Cor. 4:5, Matt. 5:11-12, Rev. 2:10, James 1:12, Rev. 6:9-11, Matt. 10:40-42, Luke 14:12-14, Heb. 6:10, 1 Thess. 2:19-20, Mark 9:41, Luke 6:32-33, Acts 10:4, Col. 3:23-25, Rom. 12:1, John 5:19, 2 John 7-8, Rev. 2–3, 2 Tim. 4:8, Luke 12:35-48, Mark 13:32-37

Chapter Four

Titus 3:14: "Our people must learn to devote themselves to doing what is good, in order that they may provide for daily necessities and not live unproductive lives."

Heb. 2:1, Ecc. 3:1-8, 11

Chapter Five

Philippians 1:10-11: "So that you may be able to discern what is best and may be pure and blameless until the day of Christ, filled with the fruit of righteousness that comes through Jesus Christ—to the glory and praise of God."

Phil. 4:9, 1 Tim. 1:2, 18, 2 Tim. 1:2, 2:1, Ex. 18:17-23, Jonah 1–4, Acts 9:4, Matt. 11:28-30, Phil. 2:12-13, John 17:21

Chapter Six

2 Thessalonians 1:11: "With this in mind, we constantly pray for you, that our God may count you worthy of his calling, and that by his power he may fulfill every good purpose of yours and every act prompted by your faith."

Luke 4:18-19, Rom. 8:1, Ex. 3:11, Num. 22:13, 28, 2 Peter 2:15-16, 1 Cor. 12:7, 11, Rom. 12:3-6, Eph. 4:7-8, John 4:6-7, 1 John 4:18, Gal. 6:9

Chapter Seven

1 Timothy 4:8: "For physical training is of some value, but godliness has value for all things, holding promise for both the present life and the life to come."

Psalm 121:3-4, Gen. 2:1-4, Psalm 103:14-16

Chapter Eight

Matthew 5:11-12: "Blessed are you when people insult you, persecute you and falsely say all kinds of evil against you because of me. Rejoice and be glad, because great is your reward in heaven, for in the same way they persecuted the prophets who were before you."

Rom. 12:1-2, Eph. 6:16, 2 Cor. 10:4-5, 2 Tim. 3:16-17, Rev. 12:10, Phil. 4:8-9, Luke 15:11-32

Chapter Nine

2 Corinthians 4:16-18: "Therefore we do not lose heart. Though outwardly we are wasting away, yet inwardly we are being renewed day by

day. For our light and momentary troubles are achieving for us an eternal glory that far outweighs them all. So we fix our eyes not on what is seen, but on what is unseen. For what is seen is temporary, but what is unseen is eternal."

Rom. 12:1-2, Rev. 6:15-17, Rom. 8:6, John 16:13, 1 Tim. 6:4, Matt. 27:46, Heb. 12:14, Eph. 4:26

Chapter Ten
Colossians 4:2: "Devote yourselves to prayer, being watchful and thankful."

Matt. 22:34-40, Phil. 4:13, Gen. 2:7, John 4:23, Is. 55:11, 1 Cor. 1:27, 1 Cor. 9:25, 2 Cor. 3:18, Rom. 8:29, 1 John 3:2, Gal. 3:3, Gal. 5:22-23, John 1:1, 14, 2 Cor. 9:7, Rom. 13:12-14, Rom. 8:12, Luke 11:3

Chapter Eleven
James 2:12-13: "Speak and act as those who are going to be judged by the law that gives freedom, because judgment without mercy will be shown to anyone who has not been merciful. Mercy triumphs over judgment!"

Phil. 1:15-18, Prov. 27:17

Chapter Twelve
2 Corinthians 8:7: "But just as you excel in everything—in faith, in speech, in knowledge, in complete earnestness and in your love for us—see that you also excel in this grace of giving."

Luke 6:12, 17, Gen. 2:18, John 12:3, Matt. 25:35-36, Luke 4:18

Chapter Thirteen
Isaiah 40:10: "See, the Sovereign LORD comes with power, and his arm rules for him. See, his reward is with him, and his recompense accompanies him."

Ecc. 3:9-14, Gen. 2:15, Gen. 3:17-19, Gal. 4:6-7, Gal. 6:9, Psalm 34:18, Rom. 8:18

Chapter Fourteen

Hebrews 10:35-36: "So do not throw away your confidence; it will be richly rewarded. You need to persevere so that when you have done the will of God, you will receive what he has promised."

1 Cor. 13, Rom. 14:10-12, Rom. 8:1, John 3:17-18, Phil. 4:13, Lam. 3:22-23, Rev. 6:17, Gen. 2:18, Luke 5:17-26

Chapter Fifteen

1 Thessalonians 3:12-13: "May the Lord make your love increase and overflow for each other and for everyone else, just as ours does for you. May he strengthen your hearts so that you will be blameless and holy in the presence of our God and Father when our Lord Jesus comes with all his holy ones."

Rom. 12:1-12, Rom. 11:33-36, Matt. 24:42-47, Micah 6:8, Eph. 2:10, Matt. 11:28-30, 1 Thess. 4:16-18

renewing the heart®
Truth and Grace for Daily Living

Welcome to a Special Place Just for Women
We hope you've enjoyed this book.
Renewing the Heart, a ministry of Focus on the Family,
is dedicated to equipping and encouraging women in all facets of their
lives. Through our Web site and a variety of other outreaches,
Renewing the Heart is a place to find answers, gain support, and,
most of all, know you're among friends.

How to Reach Us
For more information and additional resources, visit our Web site at
www.renewingtheheart.com.

To request any of these resources, call Focus on the Family at
1-800-A-FAMILY (1-800-232-6459). In Canada, call 1-800-661-9800.

You may also write us at:
Focus on the Family, Colorado Springs, CO 80995

In Canada, write to: Focus on the Family,
P.O. Box 9800, Stn. Terminal, Vancouver, B.C. V6B 4G3

To learn more about Focus on the Family or to find out if we have an
associate office in your country, please visit www.family.org.

We'd love to hear from you!

Dive Into Wholeness

With Bondage-Breakers from Focus on the Family

Reclaim Your Innate Worth

Many women accept the world's messages about what we should be—young, beautiful, successful. But what does the Bible say a woman should be? *A Woman's Search for Worth* explores this confusing topic by looking at the wholeness available through a relationship with Christ. Become the confident masterpiece you were destined to be as you discover your true identity in God!

Open the Door to God

In the hearts of most women lies a "secret place" of hidden thoughts, painful experiences, and emotions you feel are better left untouched. But God has other plans. *Who Holds the Key to Your Heart?* will help set you free as you identify your pain and find hope and healing through Scripture, testimonials, study questions, and more.

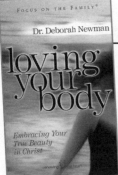

Gaze at What God Sees

Poor body image. It's the stumbling block of so many women, Christians included, who feel they never quite measure up to the world's standard of beauty. Dr. Deborah Newman's *Loving Your Body* sweeps away beauty myths to reveal the rock-solid truth about appearances. Start seeing yourself and your body the way God does!

• • •

Look for these special books in your Christian bookstore. For organizations, call 1-800-932-9123, fax 1-719-548-4654, e-mail *sales@family.org* or write to Focus on the Family, Sales Department, P.O. Box 15379, Colorado Springs, CO 80935-4654. Friends in Canada may write to Focus on the Family, P.O. Box 9800, Stn. Terminal, Vancouver, B.C. V6B 4G3 or call 1-800-661-9800.

Visit our Web site (www.family.org) to learn more about the ministry or find out if there is a Focus on the Family office in your country.